Haunted Halls of Ivy
Ghosts of Southern Colleges and Universities

Also by Daniel W. Barefoot

North Carolina's Haunted Hundred: Seaside Spectres
North Carolina's Haunted Hundred: Piedmont Phantoms
North Carolina's Haunted Hundred: Haints of the Hills
Touring the Backroads of North Carolina's Upper Coast
Touring the Backroads of North Carolina's Lower Coast
Touring North Carolina's Revolutionary War Sites
Touring South Carolina's Revolutionary War Sites
General Robert F. Hoke: Lee's Modest Warrior

Haunted Halls of Ivy

Ghosts of Southern Colleges and Universities

by
Daniel W. Barefoot

JOHN F. BLAIR, PUBLISHER
WINSTON-SALEM, NORTH CAROLINA

*The paper in this book meets the guidelines
for permanence and durability of the Committee on
Production Guidelines for Book Longevity
of the Council on Library Resources.*

Cover image -
The Chapel, University of Virginia
COURTESY OF LIBRARY OF CONGRESS, PRINTS AND PHOTOGRAPHS DIVISION,
DETROIT PUBLISHING COMPANY COLLECTION

Design by Debra Long Hampton

Library of Congress Cataloging-in-Publication Data

Barefoot, Daniel W., 1951–
Haunted halls of ivy : ghosts of southern colleges and universities / by
Daniel W. Barefoot.
p.   cm.
ISBN 0-89587-287-0 (alk. paper)
1. Haunted universities and colleges—Southern States. 2. Ghosts—
Southern States. I. Title.
BF1478.B37 2004
133.1'0975—dc22   2004014025

To my dear Kay, my college sweetheart and wife

Contents

Preface

Ghosts! Almost every college and university in the South seems to have one or two or three. In this book, you will meet the ghosts that haunt the hallowed halls of ivy in the eleven states of the old Confederacy, plus Kentucky and West Virginia.

My interest in college and university spooks grew as I researched stories for *North Carolina's Haunted Hundred*, my three-volume anthology of the haunted history of my native state. In the course of my work, it became all too apparent that the college campuses in North Carolina are among the most haunted places in the state. And the same can be said about the colleges and universities in the other states of Dixie.

Ghost stories are prevalent on Southern college campuses. Some of these stories are nothing more than tall tales or urban legends fabricated to relieve the stress of college life or to scare raw freshmen who have ventured far away from home alone for the first time in their lives.

As a native Tar Heel, I became familiar at an early age with the classic tale of the nineteenth-century haunting at the University of North Carolina at Chapel Hill. Soon after I enrolled at the historic university in 1969, I visited the site of the famous ghost story. I encountered no ghosts on my initial foray, nor have I witnessed any supernatural activities on subsequent visits to the steep cliff shadowed by eerie Gimghoul Castle. But that is not to say that those ghosts or the others on the campus of my alma mater are merely figments of vivid imaginations.

Indeed, there are a number of haunted tales from Southern colleges and universities that beg to be believed. Most of the campuses in the South are steeped in history. The nation's oldest public university and many of America's most venerable institutions of higher learning are located south of the Mason-Dixon line. These schools have survived through much of the American national experience. Where history abounds, so do ghosts.

For more than two hundred years, generation after generation of college officials and students have witnessed and reported a wide variety of supernatural forces at work on campuses from Virginia to Texas. Reliable accounts of university hauntings dating as far back as the Revolutionary War lend credence to the existence of college ghosts in the South since the days of George Washington.

Often, tragedy goes hand in hand with history to explain why a particular school is haunted. Because the South was the primary battleground of the Civil War, many of its historic schools are home to spectres lingering from the great tragedy that engulfed the entire region.

Countless students have experienced personal tragedies while attending colleges in the South. Few schools have been immune from suicides, murders, and accidental deaths. Detailed reports of subsequent paranormal experiences at the sites where those unfortunate young people died offer compelling evidence of the abiding presence of their ghosts.

Should you wish to visit one or more of the haunted campuses detailed in this volume, be mindful that they are places of higher learning. Be sure to obtain permission from each school, whether public or private, before beginning your visit.

One of the questions I am most frequently asked about my work in the field of haunted history is, "Do you believe in ghosts?" Until I began work on this book, my standard response was, "I firmly believe that there are supernatural forces at work in the world about us that cannot be explained by the laws of science."

My answer to that question changed dramatically when my wife and I visited the campus of Huntingdon College in Montgomery, Alabama, in June 2003. There, we had a personal encounter with a strange force unknown.

As the two of us made our leisurely way toward Huntingdon's picturesque Campus Green, the college grounds were devoid of students on the hot summer Sunday afternoon. Suddenly, my wife went sprawling on the sidewalk.

Dazed by the rather nasty fall, she could not walk for a few minutes. Not only did she sustain an extensive abrasion on her hand, but her left shoulder was severely bruised.

What caused her accident? My wife insists that she did not trip or stumble on the campus sidewalk in the Alabama capital. To this day, she will tell you that it was as if an invisible force pushed her from behind. No other explanation being readily available, maybe we had a rather rude introduction to Huntingdon's "Red Lady" or its "Ghost of the Green."

Do I believe in ghosts? Given our unnerving experience at Huntingdon College, my answer is a resounding yes! Perhaps you will respond in like manner after you encounter in the pages that follow the ghosts, goblins, monsters, and other supernatural entities in residence at the colleges and universities in every part of the South.

Acknowledgments

Bringing a quality book to print requires the assistance and kind offices of many individuals. Friends from far and wide have continued to provide encouragement and support to me in my quest to inform and entertain readers with tales from America's storied past. They frequently ask with great enthusiasm, "Dan, what you working on now?"

To name every person who aided me in this endeavor would be an impossible task, but there are some individuals who deserve special mention. Public-information officers at Athens State University, Florida State University, Harding University, Henderson State University, Wayland Baptist University, and the College of William and Mary provided kind and courteous responses to my inquiries. Security officers at Huntingdon College offered assistance when my wife fell on the campus.

In my hometown, Stacy Baldwin, one of my wife's students at the local high school, obtained information for me on one of her visits to her ancestral home in Grand Coteau, Louisiana.

This book is a reality due to the dedicated efforts of the staff at John F. Blair, Publisher. I am proud and honored to have this title published by Blair in the very year that the company celebrates its golden anniversary. The folks at Blair continue to work hard to produce books of high quality—a fine tradition established by the late Mr. Blair a half-century ago.

I am indebted to Carolyn Sakowski, the president of Blair, for taking a chance on an unproven author more than a decade ago and for seeing the merit in many of the ideas that I have subsequently presented. Steve Kirk, my editor at Blair, has meticulously labored over this and each of my previous manuscripts with great skill and professionalism. His advice and expertise always make for a much better book, and he is living proof of the time-honored adage, "A good editor is the author's best friend." Debbie Hampton, Anne Waters, Kim Byerly, Ed Southern, Sue Clark, and all of the others at John F. Blair have been a genuine pleasure as working partners.

My immediate family including my daughter, my mother, and my sister have been a constant source of loyalty, encouragement, and love throughout this project. While she was in Lakeland, Florida, my mother visited the campus of Florida Southern College to obtain some information for me.

But now, as in all of my past efforts, no one deserves more gratitude and praise than my wonderful wife. Once again, Kay proofed every word of the manuscript, offered suggestions to improve my prose and style, and traveled long miles with me to visit many of the haunted campuses about which you will read.

It was Kay who first suggested that I combine my love of history and my abiding interest in the supernatural to write some books about haunted history. From time to time, she reminds me of her creative idea when her shoulder twinges from her "war wound" sustained during our search for college ghosts in Alabama.

Ironically, Kay and I first caught sight of each other as college students on the campus of the University of North Carolina at Chapel Hill in 1971. We both consider that meeting as nothing short of kismet. About the time this book hits the shelves, the college sweethearts will celebrate their thirtieth wedding anniversary. It's been a supernatural romance all along the way, and I'm bewitched by the thoughts of our pleasant years together that are yet to come.

Haunted Halls of Ivy
Ghosts of Southern Colleges and Universities

The Haunts of Old Athens

Athens State University is a paradox. It is the oldest as well as the youngest school of higher education in Alabama's state educational system. Established in the northern Alabama town of Athens in 1822 as the Athens Female Academy, the college associated itself with the Methodist Church twenty-eight years later. In June 1975, the school was transferred to the state and acquired its current name.

Throughout its long history, Athens State has attracted several ghosts, one of which is perhaps the most controversial ghost in all of Alabama.

Founders Hall, the most prominent building on the compact campus, is a place of legends and spirits. Local citizens joined forces to construct the monumental four-columned structure in 1822. Indicative of the early religious influence at the school, the Corinthian columns are named Matthew, Mark, Luke, and John. At the height of the Civil War, Union troops invaded Athens and promptly threatened to put Founders

Hall to the torch. Madame Jane Hamilton Childs, the very stern and proper headmistress (whose ghost is said to roam the campus dormitories), confronted the warriors and presented their commanding officer with a note supposedly from Abraham Lincoln. With great dispatch, the invaders departed, leaving the campus intact.

In the aftermath of the war, a great tragedy that would produce the ghost of Founders Hall took place on the majestic grand staircase that leads to the second and third floors. Very late one night, two girls who lived on the upper floor of Founders decided to violate curfew and sneak out to meet their two courtiers. As the two students tiptoed down the dark staircase, they carried candles to light their way. A sudden gust of wind blew the candle flame into the hair of one of the unsuspecting young ladies. Spreading rapidly, the fire engulfed her entire body. She died as a result of the terrible conflagration.

Not long after the student's death, a supernatural presence thought to be the ghost of the burned girl took up residence in Founders Hall. Even now, disembodied footsteps are heard in many parts of the building, particularly on the grand staircase. In one room, the lights will automatically turn back on after they have been extinguished. Squeaking doors and clicking sounds have been heard when the venerable structure is devoid of human occupants. Passersby have observed a spectral form in a window on the third floor.

Building employees have detected unusual cold spots and have experienced sudden gusts of chilly air. While burning the midnight oil in his office at Founders, one professor noted the sound of jingling keys in a nearby corridor. Concerned about the disturbance, he opened his door only to find a foglike apparition standing before him.

While visiting the campus for a job interview, another professor spent the night in the residential quarters of Founders. When the creepy sounds of rattling chains and phantom footsteps awoke him from a peaceful slumber, the terrified man left the campus, never to return.

Just east of Founders stands Brown Hall, the office of the university president. Constructed in 1912, the building honors the life and memory of Florence Brown, a heroine who served as the president's secretary in the early twentieth century. When a typhoid epidemic swept through Athens in 1909, the entire faculty fled the campus. Florence Brown remained behind to minister to the female students who were suffering from the disease. Sadly, the kindly nurse and all of her patients succumbed to the deadly malady while quartered in Brown Hall.

At night, strange, inexplicable things are said to take place in the building. Objects left at day's end are found in different places at the beginning of the next workday. An instructor who once taught continuing-education classes in Brown witnessed a supernatural chain reaction there one evening. After a picture abruptly fell from the wall, a trash can began a bizarre knocking sound. Then, around the entire room, all manner of things went haywire, almost in domino succession, until calm finally returned.

And there is McCandless Hall, the site of the most famous haunting at Athens State. That a ghost inhabits the campus auditorium is not in dispute. However, a controversy has developed in recent years as to the identity of the person represented by the McCandless ghost.

Since the night in 1914 when the building was dedicated, folks on the Athens campus have reported seeing the ghostly form of a young lady in a formal white dress in and about McCandless. This apparition, holding flowers, has been frequently observed casting a strange light from the third floor. Some students have smelled her flowers. Others have seen the ghost in the dressing rooms, as if she were preparing for a performance. Her phantom footsteps have been heard throughout the stately old structure.

For more than half a century, no one questioned the identity of the McCandless ghost. On that opening night back in 1914, Abigail Lylia Burns, a lovely actress and singer with beautiful blond hair, was said to have brought the house down with her magnificent soprano voice. After receiving a standing ovation, Miss Burns concluded her performance by vowing to return. Alas and alack! Later that evening, while en route to her home, Miss Burns ran headlong into a violent thunderstorm. Her horse panicked, causing her buggy to overturn. The radiant, budding star was killed instantly. Not long after her death, the ghost of McCandless began making its appearances, and it was generally presumed that Miss Burns had kept her promise to return.

But then in 1997, Mark Durm, a professor at Athens State, published his research indicating that there were no existing death records for Abigail Burns. Instead, Durm's findings indicated that the opening-night performers at McCandless included the college glee club, opera star Enrico Aresoni, and the Zoeller String Quartet of Brussels.

Despite the attempts to debunk the Abigail Burns ghost story, there are some people who refuse to believe that the McCandless revenant is any other than that of the girl. A memorial concert for Miss Burns was held at the nearby Huntsville Opera Theater in the late twentieth century. It attracted several hundred people who hoped to witness her ghost. Several detected a supernatural presence.

Who or what haunts McCandless Hall? No answer to the mystery will likely be forthcoming. After all, when the spectral lady of McCandless or any of the other ghosts in the old buildings on the Athens State University campus are encountered, no one is willing to tarry long enough to ask for a name.

Sydney

Throughout the South, one of the most haunted sites on many college campuses is the theater. Since the mid-1920s, the theater of Auburn University has had but two homes. The buildings have one thing in common—a ghost by the name of Sydney.

To understand this haunting presence on the Alabama plains at Auburn, you must know something about Sydney the man. Sydney was Sydney Grimlett, a young, swashbuckling English cavalier who sailed across the Atlantic after the outbreak of the Civil War to offer his services to the Confederate States of America. When Union general William T. Sherman began his rampage across Georgia in the summer of 1864, Captain Sydney Grimlett of the Sixth Virginia Cavalry was one of the thousands of Confederates interposed against the marauding Yankees. In the course of the horrific fighting that followed, the bold

English officer was seriously wounded when a piece of artillery shrapnel struck his leg.

For medical treatment, the fallen soldier was transported to the makeshift Confederate hospital facilities in Auburn Presbyterian Church at the corner of College Street and Thatch Avenue. Dr. A. L. Bryan promptly examined him and dressed Sydney's wound in an attempt to save not only the life but also the leg of the gallant volunteer. Despite the efforts of the talented surgeon, gangrene set in, and he was left with no alternative. During the ensuing amputation, Sydney bled to death.

Because of the exigencies of war, the body could not be shipped to England for burial by Sydney's family and friends. Instead, a plot at nearby Pine Hill Cemetery was prepared for his interment alongside the graves of many unidentified Southern warriors. There, Sydney was laid to his final rest—or so thought the folks of Auburn.

For almost sixty years, Sydney Grimlett was little more than a sad memory of the tragic war that had brought death and destruction to the South. As for the building where he died, the local Presbyterians moved to a new church after it was completed in 1917. Four years later, they sold their former church building to Auburn University. A decade following the acquisition, the school's Theater Department moved in when its quarters on the fourth floor of Samford Hall were condemned. That was when strange things started happening.

No one really knows what prompted Sydney's spirit to come to life when the actors took over the old church premises. Speculation is that he did not like the accents of the thespians who performed an English play soon after taking up residence in the building in 1926. Others believe that the British drama made Sydney's spirit homesick for his native land. Whatever the reason, the ghost of Sydney Grimlett quickly and emphatically made his presence known. Actors and technicians detected a whistling sound and the rhythmic tapping of a foot in the attic. Scenery was moved without explanation during the night. Props frequently malfunctioned without apparent cause.

During the production of *Long Day's Journey into Night*, a bizarre light not produced by the technical staff was observed floating above the stage. And then it happened! Several theater students saw what appeared to be the apparition of a man.

Anxious to confirm the identity of the supernatural being, the students consulted a Ouija board, which reportedly indicated that the source of the strange disturbances was none other than Sydney Grimlett.

Generations of Auburn students developed an affection for their resident ghost. In 1971, the Telfair Peet Theater, a 45,534-square-foot state-of-the-art drama complex, was completed to replace the old church building as the home of the Theater Department. In order to induce Sydney's ghost to move with them, students left behind a written invitation with directions to the new facility. And to make the spirit feel welcome in his new home, the Auburn Players chose to name the award for the most outstanding drama student the Sydney Award.

Sydney kindly accepted the invitation, and his spirit is very much in evidence in the Peet Theater, where weird, unexplainable noises are the rule rather than the exception. For example, the administrative secretary of the theater was closing down the otherwise empty building one afternoon when she heard three knocks on the wall. No prankster or other apparent source of the knocks was ever found. Then there was the theater major from Buffalo, New York, who was doing some electrical work late one evening in preparation for an upcoming performance. Suddenly, his attention was drawn to a rattling sound that seemed to originate in the air conditioner. Maintenance employees were summoned, but they could find no malfunction. When the student once again heard the rattle, he noticed that the air conditioner was not running.

Some drama students and theater personnel have heard music coming from a piano not being played by human hands. Two coeds working on a project in a classroom at the Peet Theater during predawn hours heard the unmistakable sound of coins rolling down the hallway. Their curiosity aroused, the girls walked out into the corridor, only to find nothing and no one there.

On a regular basis, drawers open and close at will, lights turn on and off without a human touch, and props mysteriously disappear, only to reappear in different places. Students and backstage workers have noticed that Sydney has a great fondness for shoes in the costume department.

Sydney's spectral form has been observed in at least three parts of the building. A quartet of students working late one night in the costume shop suddenly noticed the reflection of a person in the door window. They estimated the image to be approximately five and a half feet tall. A thorough search of the locked building yielded no other human being.

While dressing for performances, some actors have heard footsteps going up and down the empty stairs to the costume shop.

In the greenroom, where performers congregate before they go on stage, Sydney's presence has caused lockers to shake and tremble uncontrollably. And in the adjacent corridor, more than one person has come face to face with the apparition of Captain Grimlett.

The ghost's favorite haunt appears to be the catwalks above the stage. His shadowy form has been observed there during countless rehearsals and at the debut of new productions. Theater staffers often leave chocolate candies (he's partial to peanut M&M's) on the catwalks for Sydney's benefit. The confections always seem to mysteriously disappear.

Sydney's former home, now listed on the National Register of Historic Places, currently serves as the university chapel. His present home is an outstanding venue where you can watch Auburn students showcase their flair for the dramatic. If you happen to catch a Shakespearean play here, take a close look at the actors, for Sydney has been observed practicing his Shakespeare on the Telfair Peet stage.

The Red Lady

The sight of a beautiful lady attired in a stunning, bright red evening dress can evoke thoughts of glamour and romance. In 1987, British pop-rock singer Chris DeBurgh expressed those sentiments in his top-ten hit ballad, "Lady in Red."

Conversely, spectral ladies in red have long evoked a more sinister, frightening connotation. And so it is with the Red Lady of Huntingdon College in Montgomery, Alabama.

Huntingdon, a small liberal-arts school long associated with the United Methodist Church, has a student body of six hundred. In 1935, the college acquired its present name to honor Selina, countess of Huntingdon, one of the first women of influence in the Wesleyan movement. But the roots of the institution and its ghost can be traced to Tuskegee in upstate Alabama, where the school was chartered and established as Tuskegee Female College in 1854. One dark night, just after "lights out" at Sky Alley (as the upper floor of the school's residence hall was known), an eerie red light made its way through the cracks of the doors lining the corridor. Some of the bravest and most curious young ladies on the hall peeped from their rooms, only to behold a rather startling sight: the apparition of a lady wearing an exquisite red gown and carrying a red parasol. She radiated a bright red light that bathed the hallway with its glow.

Seemingly oblivious to the young women she had terrified, the Red Lady glided up and down the corridor, her head and eyes always fixed forward. For the duration of that night—which to the eyewitnesses of the supernatural spectacle was interminable—the relentless pacing continued. Finally, when dawn's first light began to break, the mortified students, clustered in a single room for comfort and society, breathed a collective sigh of relief when the wraith vanished.

Unnerved by the experience, the girls of Sky Alley retired each night thereafter with an intense fear that the Red Lady would make another visit. She never returned to the Tuskegee campus, and there was never any satisfactory explanation for the haunting.

When the campus was relocated to Montgomery in 1910, the school was renamed the Woman's College of Alabama. At that time, few people gave the Red Lady any thought. She was simply a thing of the past. That is, until Margaret came along.

Margaret was a quiet, introverted young lady who enrolled at the new Montgomery campus at the behest of her family. Her parents, both natives of Alabama, had moved to New York prior to Margaret's birth, and it was in the North where the girl had been reared in an atmosphere of affluence. Margaret's grandmother had graduated from Huntingdon when it was located in Tuskegee, and her father's will contained specific instructions that Margaret should attend the college.

Margaret did not want to go to school at Huntingdon. Her heart was not in it. After all, she was a New Yorker, and Alabama was an alien place to her. But it seemed that she had no alternative, and so she acceded to the wishes of her elders.

When she arrived on campus, Margaret drew attention because of her strange fondness for things red. She always wore red clothes. And her dormitory room on the fourth floor of Pratt Hall was decorated in but one color—red. Her bedspread, her rug, her curtains, and her accessories were all red.

At Huntingdon, Margaret was an outsider. She was shy and thus did not make friends with the girls on her hall. Most of them considered her a wealthy snob and went out of their way to avoid her. When fellow students came to visit her roommate, they ignored the withdrawn girl, and she them. But they could not refrain from eyeballing the sea of crimson on Margaret's side of the room. Because no one had established a relationship with the loner, no explanation was forthcoming for her obvious obsession with a single color.

As time passed, the sullen atmosphere that pervaded the room was more than Margaret's roommate could take. Her request for a room change was granted, and she moved out. Margaret's next roommate lasted but a week. Over the ensuing weeks, roommates came and went as the eccentric girl in red grew more reclusive.

In an attempt to resolve the growing crisis on the fourth floor, the president of Pratt Hall, widely recognized and admired for her congenial nature, agreed to become Margaret's roommate. Try as she might to foster a genuine friendship with the morose, embittered young woman, the dorm president made no headway. When the grim situation began to threaten her emotional stability, the well-intentioned lady assembled her belongings in preparation for moving from the room, which was located at the isolated end of the hall.

Margaret walked in just as the dorm president was making her way to the door. Taken aback by what was going on, the strange lady in red bitterly confronted her roommate. She told her to leave, accused her of being just like the others, and warned her that she would forever regret her decision to move out.

Following the rather nasty showdown, no resident of Pratt dared to share a room with Margaret, whose mere presence, it was said, caused a chill in the air. Thereafter, Margaret could most often be found in the loneliness of her room, shrouded in her red bed covering.

Then, suddenly, her behavior changed from the melancholy to the abhorrent and frightening. Once the call of "lights out" was sounded, Margaret walked out into the corridor and proceeded to make her way into each room on the floor. Not once did she utter a word or a sound. Rather, she only cast a trancelike stare. Night after night, she paced the hall and opened and closed the doors of the other residents at will.

When Margaret failed to show up in the classroom and dining hall one day, the dorm president felt compelled to check on her former room-mate. Drawing closer to the room at the terminus of the corridor, she was startled to observe what countless Huntingdon students who followed her were to see. A strange red glow was emanating from Margaret's transom.

When the door was opened, the concerned girl witnessed a ghastly sight. Margaret's lifeless body, dressed in a red robe and cloaked with her red bedspread, was sprawled on the floor in a pool of blood. She had bled to death after slashing her wrists.

The dorm president gave a horrific scream that pierced every room on the fourth floor. She fainted before the other residents could arrive to ascertain the cause of the commotion.

Following her death by suicide, Margaret—or at least her ghost—has never left the fourth floor of Pratt. Generations of Huntingdon students have witnessed the ghostly lady in red quietly making her way up and down the hall. Dorm residents have been found cowering in abject fear after witnessing the apparition pass through closed doors and solid walls.

Huntingdon students claim that on the anniversary of Margaret's death, the supernatural activities seem to increase. Her ghost always appears on that night, and the strange red light glows from her former room.

For what reason does Margaret's spirit remain in residence at Pratt? Perhaps she wants to warn other students not to mistreat or reject their peers. Former occupants of the fourth floor indicate that they never felt as if they were alone on the hall. There was the bizarre feeling that someone or something was around when no one else was there. On occasion, when a resident had a negative thought about a fellow student, the lights would suddenly dim and a chilly burst of air would come ripping through the room. If a student picked on another in a mean-spirited fashion, unexplainable creaking noises would fill the room.

Did the Red Lady at Tuskegee foreshadow Margaret's arrival at the Montgomery campus in the next century? Was Margaret the old Tuskegee ghost made flesh? We'll never know for sure.

Over the years, many changes have come to old Huntingdon College. Male students have long been welcomed to what began as a school for women. Stately Pratt Hall, constructed in 1912, is no longer a dorm. It is now home to the Department of Education and Psychology. The fourth floor houses the offices of the campus sororities, as well as the ghost of a student who, ironically, was never able to develop a sisterhood with her fellow students.

Should you care to visit Pratt Hall, it is located in the center of the fifty-eight-acre campus adjacent to Flowers Hall, the Gothic centerpiece of the college. En route, you will walk over or by the spectacular Campus Green, designed by the famous Olmsted brothers. Be forewarned! If, while traversing this magnificent landscape, you feel someone tug at your clothes or muss your hair or blow in your ear, it's probably only Huntingdon's Ghost of the Green. But that's yet another story from this pretty little campus that has long been the domain of the Red Lady.

Haints of War and Reconstruction

Few university campuses in the South were more directly impacted by the Civil War than the University of Alabama. In the aftermath of the bloodshed and destruction, very little was left of the state's first public university, which had opened its doors in Tuscaloosa in the spring of 1831. It is little wonder, then, that the campus is haunted by the ghosts of some of the people who walked its grounds during those turbulent times.

In 1860, the University of Alabama became a veritable military academy, not because of the looming hostilities between the North and South but as a result of a decision by the trustees. They reasoned that military dress and regulations would help to curtail the undisciplined and obnoxious student behavior then plaguing the campus. Such a change could not have come at a more opportune time for the Confederacy. During the course of the war, the University of Alabama gained the soubriquet

"West Point of the South." To the Southern war effort, it provided seven generals, twenty-five colonels, twenty-one majors, 125 captains, 273 staff and commissioned officers, and 294 private soldiers.

One of the ghostly reminders of the Civil War activities on the campus is the Little Round House, located adjacent to the Gorgas Library. In 1860, Dr. Lander C. Garland, president of the university, ordered the construction of the octagonal sentry box of gray stone. From that small building, student guards monitored campus activities.

On March 29, 1865, as the war was nearing its end, Brigadier General John T. Croxton left the Birmingham area with fifteen hundred Federal troops. He was under orders to proceed directly to Tuscaloosa, where he was "to destroy the bridge, factories, mills, university, and whatever else may be of benefit to the rebel cause." When the approach of the invading troops was detected just after midnight on April 4, the alarm was sounded on campus.

Colonel James T. Murfree, commandant of the university cadets, rushed his boys—who averaged between fifteen and sixteen years of age—into action. After a brief skirmish east of the intersection of University Boulevard and Greensboro Avenue, the outnumbered students retreated to the campus, where they promptly destroyed munitions, replenished their haversacks, and made haste out of town. Only two of their number remained behind to serve as a welcoming party for the Yankee visitors to the university.

One of the young cadets secreted himself in the Little Round House while the other strolled the university grounds as hordes of blue-jacketed soldiers made their appearance. Helplessly, this second cadet watched as the invaders followed their orders by putting fire to the university. As the flames roared, several of the Union cavalrymen approached the cadet and inquired as to where they could obtain a drink. Their accommodating host rather cheerfully informed the warriors they would find whiskey in the Little Round House.

Hurrying to the shuttered guardhouse, the thirsty Yankees smashed in the door, only to be greeted by the flaming guns of the cadet in hiding. No one else heard the hail of gunfire because at that very moment

General Croxton's forces detonated the powder magazine on campus. Amid the confusion surrounding the great explosion, the cadet fled the Little Round House and joined his comrade in a successful escape. They left in their wake three dead Yankees.

Today, the Little Round House appears much as it did on that April day in 1865. And the three Union soldiers, or their ghosts, are still there. Students and campus visitors alike are often frightened by the moans they hear and the soldierly apparitions they see at or near the old guardhouse.

Other military spectres of the Civil War era roam the nearby buildings and grounds. On the famous university quad, three spooky figures are often observed late at night, particularly when there is a low-hanging mist or in the aftermath of a dust storm. One of the apparitions is attired in a Confederate admiral's hat, and the other two appear to be rather corpulent. Some university historians have concluded that the ghost with the military hat is that of Colonel Murfree. Perhaps the revenant continues to maintain a vigil over the students, just as the commandant did so many years ago.

A spectre clad in military garb has likewise been observed patrolling the floors of Woods Hall at night. No one knows for sure, but this ghost may also be that of Commandant Murfree.

In 1867, when work began on rebuilding the university, only seven buildings stood as survivors of the horrific conflagration ignited by the Yankee marauders. In addition to the Little Round House, several of the other antebellum structures are haunted.

When constructed in 1844, Maxwell Hall housed the only observatory west of the Appalachians. Now home to the computer-based honors program, the handsome building retains its copper dome and telescope pedestal, as well as the wraith of a nineteenth-century professor whose house stood nearby.

Located in the center of the thousand-acre campus is the Gorgas House, built around 1829. Now a museum, the two-story structure originally served as the dining hall. It bears the name of Josiah Gorgas (1818-83), a renowned Confederate general who subsequently served a brief stint as president of the University of Alabama. He and his family once resided in the house where his ghost now dwells.

Ironically, Josiah Gorgas was a native of Pennsylvania. He served with distinction as an officer in the United States Army from his graduation from West Point in 1841 until 1860, when he volunteered for service in the Confederate army. His decision was primarily the result of his marriage in 1853 to Amelia Gayle Gorgas, a native of Alabama.

Recognizing the remarkable talents of Gorgas, Jefferson Davis appointed him the chief of ordnance of the Confederacy. Through his outstanding leadership, Gorgas developed an extraordinary system of acquisition, manufacture, and distribution that kept Southern soldiers well supplied with arms and munitions for much of the four-year conflict.

Following his postwar tenure as president of the University of the South, Gorgas assumed the presidency of the University of Alabama in 1878. When, six months later, a stroke rendered him unable to continue his duties as president, the trustees appointed him university librarian and gave him use of the residence that now bears his name.

Visitors and employees at the Gorgas House often hear the old soldier's ghost as he walks up and down the stairs of the dwelling where the general died. His phantom sword frequently bangs against the wall during the ghostly meanderings.

Josiah's wife, Amelia, is also alive and well in spirit form on the campus. Following her husband's death in 1893, Mrs. Gorgas assumed the position of university librarian. Until her retirement more than twenty years later, she worked tirelessly to increase the library's collection, which had been completely destroyed by General Croxton's charges. In 1937, the university named its newly completed (and current) main library in honor of Mrs. Gorgas. Even now, the ghost of the dedicated woman keeps tabs on the Amelia Gayle Gorgas Library.

The library's elevators can be programmed so that they will not stop at the special-collections division on the fourth floor. Nevertheless, there is one elevator that runs of its own accord, despite its programming. Fourth-floor employees have watched the door open, only to disclose an empty car. Suddenly, it will close and the elevator will be under way again. No other explanation being readily available, the bizarre occurrences are attributed to the wraith of Amelia Gorgas, who continues to keep the place in order after all these years.

Smith Hall is home to the ghost who best represents the spirit of the university during its postwar reconstruction. Completed as the first campus building of the twentieth century, the Classical Revival structure now houses the Alabama Museum of Natural History and bears the name of Eugene Allen Smith (1841-1927), the longtime state geologist.

When Federal forces sacked the campus, they destroyed the carefully labeled collection of gems and minerals held by the university. Over a career that spanned a half-century, Eugene Smith subsequently combed the length and breadth of Alabama to discover, research, map, and collect samples of the state's natural resources. His work provided the nucleus of the highly regarded museum housed in Smith Hall.

Eugene Smith was nearing seventy years of age when he went to work in the new building that bore his name. Until his death seventeen years later, the kindly gentleman took great delight in serving as a tour guide for innumerable school groups. He was in his element while lecturing the youngsters or fielding their questions. Some say that his ghost continues to revel in the same activities.

Late one night in the mid-twentieth century, an instructor was working on his dissertation on the building's first floor—where Eugene Smith's laboratory was located—when he was disturbed by unusual noises. Certain that he was alone in the building, he quickly made his way to the second floor to ascertain the source of what sounded like a group of schoolchildren being escorted through the museum. There were indistinct voices and countless footsteps.

He found no one in the museum. To the third floor of the building he went, with the same result. Where had all those people gone? Frightened by the incident, the instructor collected his work and abruptly departed Smith Hall.

Over the years, many others associated with the building have had similar experiences. Long after closing hours, when the structure is locked tight, reliable graduate students have heard children and the voice of an adult similar to that of a tour guide, lecturer, or teacher. No human source of the phantom sounds has ever been found.

Dr. Smith first came to the Tuscaloosa campus as a student in 1860. His education was interrupted while he served the Confederacy as a captain. In 1871, he came home to the university as a professor. And he's never left. Apparently, his ghost leads phantom children on museum tours after the sun goes down.

On your visit to Tuscaloosa, whether you encounter the spirit of old Dr. Smith in his museum, the spectre of Josiah Gorgas in his home, the wraith of Amelia Gorgas in her library, the ghosts of three Yankee soldiers at the Little Round House, or the other campus spooks, you will be haunted by supernatural reminders of the time when the University of Alabama, like much of the South, was virtually destroyed and rose again from the ashes.

The Spectral Ladies of Searcy

Searcy, a city of some twenty thousand residents located in northeastern Arkansas about fifty miles from Little Rock, has been home to various institutions of higher learning since the days of Reconstruction. When Harding College relocated from Morrilton to Searcy in 1934, it took over the twenty-nine-acre campus of the Galloway College for Women. In the process, Harding, now a university, inherited several ghosts who continue to make their presence known from time to time.

From the time Galloway College opened its doors in Searcy in 1888 until it ceased operation in 1933, the institution was known far and wide for its educational and social standards. For many years, Galloway was the largest college for women in the American Southwest. Its demise was occasioned by the economic chaos of the Great Depression and by the mysterious deaths of several students at old Gooden Hall. The spectres of those unfortunate young ladies are said to haunt the campus of Harding University today.

Without question, the most famous of the ghosts at Harding is Gertie. Galloway College was at its zenith when Gertrude, the daughter of a distinguished Southern family, was a student in residence. One dark November night, most of the other girls were already asleep in the stately three-story Gooden Hall when Gertie walked in after bidding good-night to her beau. She ascended the staircase to the third floor and then made her way down the long hallway. Her white evening dress, which she had worn for the grand party of the evening, broke the stillness with light, delicate swishes as she sashayed toward her room. But then she heard something else—a strange noise coming from the direction of the abandoned elevator shaft. As she walked briskly to ascertain the source of the commotion, the attractive young woman pulled her platinum blond hair away from her ears in an attempt to better hear the sound.

Abruptly, the slumbering girls were awakened by a bloodcurdling scream that penetrated the thick walls of Gooden Hall. From a room near the staircase, the first student to peek out into the hallway was frightened when an ominous, dark form stormed past her and disappeared into the stairwell. In an instant, screaming girls poured into the corridor, while the unnerved housemother summoned the police.

When some of the more fearless girls peered down into the old elevator shaft, they quickly lost their composure. Sprawled at the bottom of the shaft was the corpse of Gertie.

Many of Gertie's friends found it hard to believe she was dead. Even in death, she looked as if she were alive. One student commented, "Why, Gertie would never get old, much less die. She would always be beautiful, young, and vibrant."

Gertie was laid to rest in the elegant gown in which she was attired on the night she died.

Years passed. Then, around 1950, a freshman awoke from a deep sleep and took a midnight stroll down the dimly lit first-floor corridor of Gooden Hall for a drink of water. Through the window at the end of the hallway, moonbeams poured in to provide an unsettling light. Perhaps it was because of the many stories that she had heard, but for some unknown reason, the young lady peeped into the boarded-up entrance to the elevator shaft. She attempted to scream, but the fright that overcame her temporarily robbed her of the ability to make a sound. Rushing back to the relative safety of her room, the tearful girl managed to stammer a few words to her roommate: "I could see her in the moonlight, sitting there in a white evening gown, combing her platinum blond hair!" Then she fainted.

Amid the developing confusion, another freshman, also an eyewitness to the apparition, cowered against a corridor wall, her eyes filled with fear. When friends tried to console her, all she could mutter was, "She, she walked right through the wall."

In a desperate attempt to quell the growing disturbance, the dean of women made her way to Gooden. She gathered the terrified girls and escorted them to the entrance of the old shaft, where she invited them to look through the boards. "Why, there's nothing down there, silly, except an old comb someone dropped," she said.

In the early 1930s, in the twilight of Galloway College, another tragedy that would have ghostly consequences unfolded at Gooden Hall. A music student who for the purposes of this story will be known as Fran was deeply in love with a young man who attended a nearby college. Late one night, her boyfriend was killed in a horrendous automobile accident. Upon receiving the devastating news, Fran was crushed. Overcome with despondency, sorrow, and despair, the mopish girl turned to her only solace in life—music.

Efforts by her friends to comfort Fran were to no avail. She preferred the loneliness of a room on the third floor of Gooden, where she continuously played a piano. Over and over and over again, Fran performed the same sad, gloomy pieces as if she were possessed.

Days passed, and the semester wore on. Finally, students found Fran dead in the room where she performed her melancholy tunes. There was no apparent cause for her death, but all of her friends concurred that she had perished of a broken heart.

Not long after Fran passed away, residents and staff at Gooden Hall began to hear the sounds of a piano emanating from the third floor late at night. Curious as to who might be playing at such an unusual hour, college officials went to the room. To their dismay, there was no one at the piano or in the room. For as long as Gooden Hall stood, the late-night phantom music recitals continued. Those familiar with the story of Fran knew the source of the nocturnal concerts. Her ghost was playing a supernatural dirge in memory of the love she had lost.

During the first decades of Harding's occupancy of the campus in Searcy, sprawling, dark Gooden Hall stood as a brooding landmark about which many strange stories were told. Students who walked past the structure often complained of the feeling that someone or something was watching them.

Then came odd reports from the building that a voice could be heard singing haunting melodies late at night. Thorough searches of Gooden found no source of the mysterious vocalist. One evening, the curiosity of a female music student was piqued when she heard the nocturnal singing. Vowing to solve the mystery once and for all, the brave coed gathered a group of friends and returned to the imposing edifice. Her friends refused to join the daring young lady as she entered Gooden. Minutes later, as they watched and waited outside, the haunting refrains echoing from the building changed to a terrifying shriek. From a second-story window emerged the terrified coed, her hands pulling out her own hair as she jumped to her death.

In the early 1950s, Gooden Hall was razed in the name of progress. Or maybe it was taken down in hopes of closing the book on its dark history. The bricks from the storied structure were salvaged and used in the construction of a new music building and an adjacent walkway.

Erected just several hundred yards from the site of Gooden, the Claud Rogers Lee Music Building apparently became the new home of some of the ghosts of old Gooden. There are numerous accounts of encounters with and sightings of Gertie in the Lee Building. Familiar with the stories of her ghost, a group of audio-engineering students locked themselves into a recording booth in the Lee Building one night to determine if the tales had any credibility. Around one o'clock in the morning, unexplainable things began to occur. Footsteps in the otherwise empty building were heard and recorded by the astonished young men.

Others familiar with the building have observed doors that open and close without human assistance. And there is also the phantom music. Workers and students on the second floor of the building have heard piano music coming from the third floor on dark nights. The building has but two floors!

In 1998, Harding University, now a school of some five thousand students, moved its Music Department from the Lee Building to the new Donald W. Reynolds Center for Music and Communication. No one knows if Fran's ghost will migrate to the $6.2 million complex to perform her *musique macabre*.

As for Gertie, it appears that her spirit will maintain its ties to the site of that tragic night long ago. Should you take a late-night stroll on the sidewalk connecting the Lee Building to the site of old Gooden, you might just have company, for more than once, a beautiful ghostlike lady wearing a shimmery white gown has been seen walking back and forth on the very bricks that long ago comprised the building where she lived and died.

HENDERSON STATE UNIVERSITY
ARKADELPHIA, ARKANSAS

The Lady in Black

Arkadelphia, located on the banks of the Ouachita (pronounced Wash-uh-taw) River in southwestern Arkansas, is a small, picturesque college town. In fact, since 1890, it has been the home of two colleges that have grown into highly respected universities. Today, Henderson State University and Ouachita Baptist University coexist in Arkadelphia as friendly rivals. But it has not always been that way. Differences between the two student bodies in the distant past produced the revenant known as the Lady in Black, who continues to haunt the Henderson State campus to this very day.

Ouachita Baptist University is the older of the two schools, having opened its doors in Arkadelphia in 1886. Its affiliation with the Baptist Church has remained strong throughout its history. On the other hand,

Henderson State, four years the junior of Ouachita, was the child of the Methodist Church. Not until 1929 did it become a public university. Values and beliefs often clashed in the early days of the two schools. And so it was with Joshua, Jane, and their friends.

In the early 1920s, Joshua enrolled at Henderson State (then known as Henderson-Brown College) filled with ambition. The handsome young man already had his life planned: he would become an attorney, then he would be elected district attorney, and ultimately he would be selected a justice of the United States Supreme Court.

As he went about obtaining the education necessary to realize his dreams, Jane came along and stole his heart.

It was an unlikely romance. After all, Jane was a student at Ouachita. And unlike Joshua, the great pragmatist, Jane was subject to flights of fancy. She was more the artist. Her dream was to become a great novelist.

Differences aside, Jane was beautiful, there was no mistaking that. Joshua fell madly in love with her. Although in those days it was almost taboo for a Henderson student to date a Ouachita student, Joshua and Jane began to see each other on a regular basis and in public settings.

Greatly concerned about the relationship, Joshua's friends at Henderson attempted to dissuade the unflappable fellow from going out with the girl from the crosstown rival. They warned him that Jane's highstrung, odd personality would prove to be a detriment to the realization of his career goals. Some said she even had a strange, dark side, citing her great fondness for horror stories, and the tales of Poe in particular.

Day after day, Joshua came back to the Henderson campus after an outing with Jane only to be greeted by his colleagues with a harangue about why he was wrong to continue seeing his Ouachita belle. Finally, their incessant pleas and constant entreaties evolved into hazing, and thus Joshua relented. He would stop seeing Jane.

When the two lovers had their next meeting, Joshua's sad words pierced Jane's heart like the sharpest of arrows. After she gained a measure of composure, the forlorn young woman tearfully pleaded that she could never marry anyone other than Joshua, and that she could not—

would not—live without him. Moved by the tenderness of the moment, Joshua mellowed a bit. Perhaps they should just spend some time apart. He then promised to take Jane to the homecoming dance at Henderson. Maybe their problems could be worked out.

Though Jane departed in great sadness, she was also filled with hope for the future. She promptly proceeded to assemble a most glamorous wardrobe for the dance. Everything—shoes, hat, veil, gloves—was to be a perfect match for the stunning black gown she would wear. Unquestionably, she would be the most beautiful lady in attendance at the elegant function, and Joshua would never again harbor any doubts that they were meant for each other.

Forces were already at work that would dash Jane's hopes and dreams. During what was supposed to be a temporary separation from Jane, Joshua met another. And this new someone attended Henderson.

When the big night finally arrived, Jane was radiant. Attired in nothing but black, she waited and waited for Joshua, who never came. Fretful that some misfortune had befallen him, the young lady hurried over to the Henderson campus. There, she found Joshua. He was fine. But all was not well.

Joshua was passionately kissing another girl. When their romantic embrace ended, they walked away hand in hand toward the homecoming dance. Tears marred the perfect makeup on Jane's face as her happiness turned to despair in the dark night.

Convinced that she had nothing for which to live, the weeping girl made her way to the steep cliffs overlooking the Ouachita River. Without hesitation, she took a leap and plunged to her death.

Some accounts say that Joshua was never the same after that fateful night. He tried to concentrate on his studies, to no avail. He tried to sleep, but a screaming lady clad in black seemed to come to him in a dream night after night.

And what about Jane, or her spirit? At each homecoming weekend on the Henderson State campus since her tragic death, her ghost, known as the Lady in Black, is said to have made an appearance. Countless people have witnessed the faint apparition of a lady clad in black floating about the campus on those nights.

Jane's ghost makes its way in and out of campus residence halls in an apparent search for something or someone. Maybe she is looking for the girl who came between Joshua and her. Or perhaps she is searching for the young man who stole her heart and then broke it.

One Henderson coed who had a close encounter with the phantom lady on the campus grounds observed that the spectre wore a black veil and emitted an eerie glow.

On another occasion, a terrifying experience in one of the residence halls left several students with lasting memories of Jane's ghost. They entered the elevator on the fourth floor and pressed the first-floor button. When the door closed, the car suddenly went to the second floor, where it abruptly stopped. Then it made its way up to the fifth floor. Finally, it descended to the third floor, where the door began to repeatedly open and close.

Slipping out of the uncontrollable elevator, the frightened students made haste to the stairwell for their descent to the first floor. As they neared the second-floor landing, the stairwell lights momentarily went out. Just when the lights came back on, a thin lady clad in a dark dress floated by the terrified group.

Television news crews have been drawn to the campus to study the homecoming phenomenon. One intrepid reporter actually went to the forbidding river cliffs where Jane ended her life. He noted that her abiding presence could almost be felt there. The site, owned by Ouachita Baptist University, is off-limits to the public.

Visitors are welcome at the two campuses that share Arkadelphia. If you plan your visit to Henderson State for a crisp, cool autumn night that just happens to be homecoming, you might encounter a lovely lady flitting about the grounds, much as she has at every homecoming since that terrible night many years ago. She's Jane, the Lady in Black.

Haunts of the Rich and Famous

St. Augustine, the oldest city in the United States, is home to one of Florida's youngest colleges. Flagler College, a liberal-arts school founded in 1968, is located on a nineteen-acre site in the heart of St. Augustine. Sprawling over an entire city block bordered by King Street, Valencia Street, Sevilla Street, and Cordova Street, the opulent former Ponce de Leon Hotel serves as the centerpiece of the Flagler campus. Henry Morrison Flagler, the man for whom the college is named, built the fabulous 540-room Ponce de Leon in 1887 from the fortune he had accumulated as a co-owner of the Standard Oil Company. Today, the ghosts of Flagler, two of his three wives, and his reputed mistress are said to haunt this ornate building, once acclaimed to be the most exclusive winter resort in America.

Flagler students live in the rooms once occupied by the socialites and high rollers of America's Gilded Age. Over the college's relatively short history, there have been numerous reports of supernatural encounters throughout the magnificent palace of Moorish Revival design. But to understand who or what the mysterious sights and sounds represent, you must have a glimpse of the life and times of Henry Morrison Flagler (1830-1913).

Flagler, the son of a small-town Presbyterian minister, aspired to a life of wealth and fame from an early age. A long-lived friendship with industrialist John D. Rockefeller took root before Henry was twenty-five years old. Shortly after the end of the Civil War, the two men formed an oil partnership that evolved into the Standard Oil Company. Henry's aspirations had been realized.

In 1883, two years after the death of Mary, his first wife, the fifty-three-year-old Flagler married Ida Alice Shrouds, eighteen years his junior. For years, she had served as a nurse for Mary Flagler, a victim of a seventeen-year illness. Ida Alice, possessed of bright blue eyes and a profusion of red hair, was best known for her vitriolic, uncontrollable temper and sudden fits of rage.

Henry took Ida Alice to Jacksonville, Florida, for their honeymoon. During their stay, the oil tycoon fell in love with St. Augustine, which at that time was devoid of a large hotel. He saw the enormous potential for developing Florida into a major tourist destination. Two years later, the Flaglers retired to St. Augustine, and Henry set about building what he called "the Newport of the South."

His first great enterprise here was the Ponce de Leon Hotel. When construction was completed in May 1887, it stood as the first major structure in the United States fabricated from poured concrete. For the interior, Flagler employed Louis Tiffany to provide the finest of glass. Murals, intricately carved wood, imported marble, Oriental carpets, and priceless furnishings were placed throughout the hotel.

In time, Flagler extended the railroad from St. Augustine down the length of Florida to Key West. Along the way, he constructed a string of a dozen fine hotels. At one point, he owned more than 3.5 million acres of land in Florida.

But money, hotels, and vast landholdings could not buy Henry Flagler happiness. By 1894, Ida Alice had begun to exhibit signs of mental illness. She is said to have been one of the first persons to purchase and use the recently invented Ouija board. Her ramblings about her impending marriage to the czar of Russia led psychiatrists to determine that she was terminally insane. In 1899, the courts concurred, and Ida Alice was institutionalized for the remaining thirty-one years of her life.

Meanwhile, Henry had fallen in love with Mary Lily Kenan, the daughter of a family long prominent in the political, military, and social history of North Carolina. In order to marry Miss Kenan, Flagler used his enormous influence to prevail upon the Florida legislature to pass a bill that made insanity grounds for absolute divorce. Once that was accomplished, Henry married Miss Kenan on August 24, 1901. He was seventy-one years old, and she was but thirty-four.

Henry Flagler died in 1913 as the result of a fall at Whitehall, the sixty-thousand-square-foot, fifty-five-room mansion he had built for his third wife in Palm Beach. His body was transported back to the rotunda of the Ponce de Leon Hotel, where it lay in state until its burial at the nearby Memorial Presbyterian Church, which Flagler had built.

While the corpse was in repose at the hotel, weird things started to happen.

All the doors and windows of the rotunda had been opened by the hotel staff, so as to allow Flagler's spirit to be freed from his body. As friends and family mourned in silence, the massive doors suddenly slammed shut without the assistance of human hands or the winds. Once the bewildered mourners regained their composure, the doors were opened by hotel employees, and the pall was promptly carried to the church.

Soon after the funeral detail made its way out of the rotunda, a sexton entered the chamber and began closing the windows and doors. In an instant, he felt an unusually strong burst of wind pass through the room, which was now tightly closed. At almost the same moment, the man glanced at the tile floor, distinguished by its intricate designs. His attention was immediately drawn to one particular tile. In it, there was a new design: a thumbnail-sized likeness of the face of Henry Flagler. To this day, the strange tile is visible. Those familiar with the bizarre incident believe that Flagler's spirit bounced off a closed window and landed on the rotunda floor. It is said to have been trapped in the old hotel when the windows and doors of the great room were closed.

One Flagler College student who walked past the unusual tile on a daily basis got more than he bargained for when he, in jest, rubbed Flagler's likeness and invited his spirit to come up to his room for a visit. Later that day, the young man was laboring at his desk when he perceived that he was not alone in his room. Turning around to look in the direction of his open door, he found no one present. Suddenly, the door closed, and the student was overwhelmed by an unnerving sensation that there was someone in the room with him. Momentarily, the door opened on its own, and things returned to normal.

Henry Flagler's ghost is not the only supernatural presence in the old hotel. Mary Lily, the third Flagler wife, died in Louisville, Kentucky, in 1917, but her wraith was witnessed by a Flagler College security guard in the early 1980s. While on duty one night in the former hotel building, he detected the unmistakable sound of footsteps on the marble staircase leading to the mezzanine. His eyes caught the blur of a white skirt as it turned the corner.

Concerned that a visitor might be in the building after hours, he sprinted toward the steps. Again, he heard the footsteps and gained a quick look at the white skirt. Once he reached the landing, he noticed that the lady had made her way into the first room on the hallway. But a search of the room yielded no human occupants. After the incident was reported, it became apparent to those familiar with the old hotel that the apparition was that of Mary Lily Kenan Flagler.

And what about Ida Alice? Her ghost is said to frequent the third floor of the former Ponce de Leon, particularly the room where she lived. Spectacular clear-glass Tiffany windows reflected beautiful prisms of sunlight into the mirrored room on the eastern front of the building, where Ida Alice gradually went mad. As her mental instability grew worse, she was often locked in the room for her own safety and for that of the other occupants of the hotel.

After the Ponce de Leon became a college dormitory, coeds who lived in Ida Alice's room experienced terrifying supernatural occurrences. Pictures and other objects attached to the walls would often be scattered about the floor when the residents returned to their room.

Ultimately, college officials decided to close the room belonging to the second Mrs. Flagler. No one lives in it to this day. From time to time, an eerie glow can be seen emanating from the cracks around the door.

Students who occupy the adjacent rooms report that no items will stay attached to the walls that are shared with the haunted room.

One particular Flagler College coed who lived in the east wing of the building bore a striking resemblance to Ida Alice. Not long after the student's arrival on campus, the apparition of Flagler's second wife was observed roaming the corridors of the east wing. Finally, it took up residence in the coed's room. On occasion, the unfortunate young woman would wake to find Ida Alice's ghost hovering over her with a cold, death-like face. At other times, the revenant would be standing in the room when the student returned from class. Unwilling to share her room with a ghost, the girl transferred to Rollins College.

Third-floor residents often complain of strange noises that drift down from the fourth floor, where the hotel's ballroom was located. The entire floor is closed to students and the public. Orchestra music, hushed voices, and footsteps have been heard coming from the floor, which is home to no one save the ghost of Henry Flagler's alleged mistress.

Those who have been witness to the phantom have described her as "the Lady in Black." As the story goes, Ida Alice showed up at the hotel unexpectedly one day while the other woman was there. Unwilling to chance the possibility that the two women might run into each other, Henry Flagler banished the other woman to an out-of-the-way room on the fourth floor. As the days passed, her despondency turned to despair, and she hanged herself. Now, the spectral Lady in Black sometimes beckons visitors from the top of the steps to the fourth floor.

Student-guided tours of portions of this majestic college building are available for a nominal fee. If you happen to be among a tour group in which an elderly man bedecked in a straw hat suddenly wanders away, don't be overly concerned. The same thing has happened before. It's only the ghost of old Henry Morrison Flagler on his daily prowl about this place where the Flagler empire in Florida was born.

Haunted Child of the Sun

*". . . out of the ground, and into the light, a child of the
sun."*

Frank Lloyd Wright

Located on the shore of picturesque Lake Hollingsworth in the central Florida city of Lakeland, Florida Southern almost became a ghost itself in its infancy. From a very modest beginning in 1883 in Orlando, the small Methodist school somehow survived four campus moves, numerous severe storms, fires, and economic crises until it found a permanent home in 1922. Today, the hauntingly beautiful hundred-acre campus boasts forty-five major buildings, some of which are inhabited by ghosts, including that of America's most famous architect, Frank Lloyd Wright.

In 1938, Wright began a long personal association with the Lakeland college at the invitation of Dr. Ludd M. Spivey (1886-1962), who served as president of Florida Southern from 1925 to 1957. Spivey, an ordained Methodist minister and a respected scholar, saved the school from closing during the economic chaos of the Great Depression by leading a one-man fund-raising campaign after the trustees had voted to close its doors. Capitalizing on his success, Spivey, a man of great energy and vision, embarked upon a mission to turn the tiny liberal-arts institution, which consisted of only a handful of buildings in 1937, into "a great education temple in Florida." To make his dream come true, he sought the expertise and assistance of Frank Lloyd Wright.

At Taliesin, the renowned architect's famous estate in Spring Green, Wisconsin, Spivey presented an intriguing proposal and challenge: "I have no money with which to build the modern American campus, but if you'll design the buildings, I'll work night and day to raise the money. Just how, I don't know, but together we can do it."

Frank Lloyd Wright was sixty-seven years old when he first saw the sixty-two-acre orange grove where his architectural masterpiece was to take shape. The site was the perfect place to build what he termed his "child of the sun." A mere handshake sealed the agreement. Wright promptly prepared a master plan wherein he envisioned a complex of eighteen separate buildings.

Construction of the first building, the Annie Pfeiffer Chapel, began in November 1938. From the outset, funding for the ambitious project was a serious problem. Because construction costs were projected to be more than four times the budgeted amount, Spivey and Wright agreed to bring the architect's plans to life with student labor.

From Taliesin, Wright dispatched several of his students to Lakeland with blueprints that bore no dimensions and few details. Once on the campus, Wright's tutees developed detailed working plans, which the Florida Southern students used to erect the buildings from basic materials: cypress, sand, and coquina, all natural to Florida; steel and concrete for strength; and glass for light.

For almost twenty years until his death in 1957, Wright remained true to his architectural concept for Florida Southern: "We ought to help the indoors to go outdoors and the outdoors to come inside." Key elements in the "real Florida form" were skylights and flat or low roofs. On one occasion, Ludd Spivey noted this about one of the buildings in a letter to Wright: "The skylight keeps leaking and I have water all over my desk. What should I do?" Wright responded, "I guess you are going to have to move your desk."

Following the retirement of President Spivey in 1957 and the subsequent death of the innovative architect, the master plan was put aside. Twelve of the eighteen buildings designed by Wright were completed. Today, they constitute the world's largest collection of Frank Lloyd Wright buildings on a single site.

When he walked about the campus that he helped design, Wright could readily be identified by his customary attire: a beret or porkpie hat and a flowing cape. During his long association with Florida Southern, the ingenious architect paid many visits to the campus. There are some people who claim that he never left.

His spirit is said to haunt the Annie Pfeiffer Chapel, the cornerstone of the campus that was born of his plan. Completed in 1941 at a cost of a hundred thousand dollars, the structure was quickly dubbed by students as "the Bicycle Rack in the Sky" and "the Bow Tie" because of its unique wrought-iron work and exterior design. Wright's supernatural presence has been experienced by students and visitors alike in the interior of the building, particularly in the loft area. According to campus tradition, the plans of the famous architect were turned upside down during the construction of the chapel, and the loft was thus not built in conformity with Wright's design. Supposedly, he was very unhappy when he observed the finished product, and his ghost is said to roam the loft trying to remedy the flaws.

Persons who have encountered the spirit in the loft have departed the building in a state of fright. In the otherwise peaceful setting, they have reported being overwhelmed by a sense of unease as they watched an oppressive mist surround them.

In other Florida Southern buildings dating both before and after the

Wright plan, ghosts and supernatural forces are also at work.

Located east of the Annie Pfeiffer Chapel in the center of the campus, the three-story Joseph-Reynolds Hall is a handsome brick dormitory. Completed in 1922 as one of the first structures on the campus, the building housed Dr. Ludd Spivey and his family for some years until a permanent residence was constructed for the college president. In 1932, Dr. Spivey's seven-year-old son, Allan, was bitten by a rabid dog. He died three weeks later. Since Allan's death, occupants of Joseph-Reynolds Hall, which currently serves as a dormitory for 243 men and women, have experienced many weird, inexplicable, and frightening occurrences.

Phantom sounds of moving furniture late at night, of footsteps on empty stairs or in a vacant hallway, and of a ball bouncing against a wall are all attributed to the ghost of the little boy. Some students and campus employees claim to have seen an angel in the building. Could it represent Allan Spivey?

A second-floor room in Joseph-Reynolds Hall is said to be haunted as a result of the tragic death of a young lady some years ago. She was killed during a spat with her lover, and her blood stained the balcony overlooking the Hindu Garden of Meditation. Maintenance personnel subsequently painted over the stains several times in an unsuccessful attempt to cover the grim reminders of the tragedy. Each time, the strange red spots reappeared. All of the upper-story balconies are now inaccessible to building residents.

Just east of Joseph-Reynolds Hall stands Allan Spivey Hall, a dormitory built in 1936-37. In the courtyard is the Spivey Memorial, a bronze urn said to contain the ashes of Allan Spivey. Tradition has it that the artist who designed the urn died a sudden and mysterious death before the cast was made. Some people have detected chilly air coming from the urn, even though it is completely sealed.

The college theater is located near the southwestern corner of the campus by the Ludd M. Spivey Fine Arts Center. An unidentified ghost frequently makes its presence known here. Many theater patrons have noticed sudden drops in temperature during performances in the auditorium. Actors and backstage personnel have been annoyed by lights that suddenly malfunction without reason during presentations, then function flawlessly after the curtain has dropped. Many a worker has become unnerved upon hearing his name called when no one was about. Some stagehands have reported the eerie sensation that they were being watched by an invisible presence. Others have heard footsteps on the empty catwalk.

And then there are the haunted passages that run underneath the campus. A veritable labyrinth of sixteen tunnels, reportedly built to protect students during World War II or to hide a Soviet scientist during the Cold War, are said to connect various college buildings. Fraternities at the college of seventeen hundred students once used the subterranean corridors as a playground. In the 1970s, a worker is believed to have disappeared in the underground complex and was never found. College officials have attempted to discredit many of the stories related to the tunnels. The director of finance said, "What the tunnels really are is a crawlspace." Whatever the case, the maintenance staff at Florida Southern has made a concerted effort to seal the entrances to the passageways.

Whether something or someone haunts the underground at Florida Southern College may never be known, but one thing is certain: the buildings at this "child of the sun" hold hauntings aplenty. You can see for yourself on the self-guided walking tour, which begins at the Frank Lloyd Wright Visitor Center on the campus. That is, if you dare!

Living with Ghosts

For many young people, college presents their first opportunity to live away from home for an extended period of time. Consequently, the decision as to where to live becomes one of great importance for a student after admission to a particular school. Physical facilities, roommates, size, and location are among the many factors that must be taken into consideration in the selection of campus housing. At Florida State, a massive university with approximately thirty-six thousand students on its Tallahassee campus, another factor should be considered in the decision about housing. Students might want to ask, "Is the place haunted?"

Completed in 1948, Cawthon Hall is one of the most architecturally pleasing dormitories at Florida State. As one of the last campus structures built in the Collegiate Gothic style, it has turrets and irregular shadows that lend a spooky aura. And in its interior, the ghosts who roam the corridors and rooms constantly remind Cawthon residents that their dorm is indeed haunted.

One of the Cawthon ghosts is said to be that of Sarah Landrum Cawthon, the woman for whom the building is named. Back in 1910, when the university was known as Florida State College for Women, Mrs. Cawthon was hired by Edward Conrad, the school's president, as a dean to serve as an adviser to the students. Her assignment was to offer guidance as to the proper and appropriate behavior of young ladies. In her additional role as housemother, Cawthon proved to be a popular and beloved mother away from home for many of the young women.

Sarah Cawthon—or "Tissie," as she was affectionately known—was ever anxious to assist her girls in their academic and social lives. But Tissie was not ready for and could not accept the behavioral changes that took place on her campus and throughout the United States during the Roaring Twenties. She watched in dismay as American women wore revealing clothing, adopted unusual hairstyles, participated publicly in smoking and drinking, and chose alternative ways of thinking and acting that were rebellious in the eyes of the establishment.

Florida State officials decided to honor the memory of this university matriarch when Cawthon Hall was dedicated in the late 1940s. At about the same time, men were first admitted to the university. Perhaps for that reason, Tissie's spirit promptly took up residence in the dorm as soon as it was completed. Since that time, her supernatural presence has been experienced by many Cawthon residents. Doors often slam shut without rational explanation, and lights turn on and off by themselves.

Several years ago, the interior of Cawthon was completely gutted for asbestos removal and modernization. As the renovation project moved along, the university issued press releases detailing the activities of Mrs. Cawthon's ghost. By all accounts, she was pleased with the facelift to her home.

At present, almost three hundred students live in the renovated dorm. Most know that there is a ghost watching over them. When Cawthon residents sense an invisible someone brush by them, feel an eerie tap on the shoulder, or hear the faint sound of a weeping woman or a phantom sigh of disgust, they understand that their demeanor must improve, for Tissie still insists on proper behavior after all these years.

Cawthon Hall is also inhabited by the ghost of a student who was killed in a freak accident not long after the dorm was completed. One bright day, the unfortunate young lady made her way to the roof of the tall building to enjoy a leisurely sunbath. As often happens on hot Florida afternoons, a thunderstorm erupted and swept toward the campus. All the while, the sky was clear blue over Cawthon Hall. Suddenly, a wicked streak of lightning—literally a bolt from the blue—struck the student atop the building. She was killed instantly.

In the aftermath of her untimely death, strange, inexplicable things began taking place in the deceased girl's room at Cawthon. To this day, they continue. When the room is securely locked during the absence of its human residents, books, pictures, and other items are mysteriously moved. At night, students dwelling in the haunted room hear eerie sounds and are often overwhelmed by the sensation that there is another being in their midst.

Students using a communal shower over at Reynolds Hall sometimes bathe with a ghost. Frequently encountered in this residence hall is the supernatural presence of a custodian who hanged himself here years ago. His wraith likes to vex Reynolds residents by opening and closing the bathroom doors and by turning the showers on and off.

Much like their counterparts at other Southern universities, many Florida State students choose to live in social fraternities and sororities. Some of the Greek houses on the Tallahassee campus are not without haunts. And these ghosts are of a more sinister nature than those in the dorms.

Without question, the most publicized crime in Florida State history took place in the wee hours of Saturday, January 15, 1978, at the Chi Omega sorority house near the university campus. While most of the members were out on dates, a few of their sisters were asleep in the house when Theodore Robert "Ted" Bundy forced his way into their bedrooms. Using a club and some pantyhose, the handsome former law student murdered two of the girls and seriously assaulted two others. His crime spree on that fateful night in Tallahassee was not his first, nor would it be his last. But it was his conviction for the two gruesome murders at the Florida State sorority that sent Ted Bundy, one of the most infamous serial killers in the annals of crime, to the electric chair on January 24, 1989.

Since the Bundy murders at Chi Omega, many of the sisters who have lived there came to believe that the ghosts of the two victims abide in the house. A strange, uneasy feeling often overcomes the residents. One sister who disavowed any belief in ghosts or things supernatural openly admitted that she experienced odd, frightening sensations in the house but at no other place.

Not every sister sleeping at Chi Omega on the night of Ted Bundy's onslaught fell prey to his brutal, deadly violence. One lucky young lady awoke in her room that night with an intense thirst. She got out of bed to get a drink of water in the hall bathroom, but as she neared her locked door, a bizarre feeling that there was a terrible evil outside swept over her. Refusing to open the door, she returned to her bed.

Ted Bundy's ghost has never been observed at Chi Omega, but the story over at the Phi Delta Theta fraternity is a bit different. Located at 409 College Avenue, the house is known as "the Oak," a reference to the millennium-old tree that graces the front yard. Before the fraternity converted the expansive structure into a chapter house, it served as a rooming house. Here, on December 31, 1977, an escaped murder suspect from Colorado took up residence. Ted Bundy fled to Tallahassee, where he convinced himself that he was free of the evil force that had caused him to murder some two dozen women. It was from this house that Bundy took the early-morning walk two weeks later that led him to the sorority house where he again killed.

Not more than two weeks after the executioner sent a lethal jolt of two thousand volts through Bundy's body at the state penitentiary in Starke, Florida, several women were passing the Oak—which by this time was occupied by the fraternity—when they noticed a shadowy figure who resembled the serial killer standing on the porch. Suddenly, he, or it, was gone. Others have since witnessed the same phenomenon at the entrance to the fraternity and on its grounds.

Located just down the street from the Oak is the Sigma Chi fraternity house. This rambling two-story structure graces the site where a nineteenth-century house once stood. It is from that old dwelling that the Sigma Chi brothers have inherited their ghost.

Sallie was a young household servant who worked in the former structure. One dark night, an intruder stole into the house and viciously attacked and assaulted her. In the course of the ensuing struggle, both the assailant and his victim died.

When Sigma Chi located its chapter house here, the brothers began to report the presence of a supernatural entity. Some saw the apparition of the murdered girl. Two of the bedrooms were filled with odd odors. One smelled like a canning pantry, while the other reeked of coal.

A paranormal expert was summoned to investigate the unusual reports. From the investigation, the fraternity members learned that the bedrooms in question were located near the summer kitchen and the coalbin of the former house. On the tragic night long ago, Sallie stabbed her attacker in the kitchen and fled to the coalbin, where the dying man found her and mustered enough strength to strangle the life from her body. To this day, the Sigma Chi brothers continue to see and sense the presence of their ghosts.

Florida State University offers a wide array of alternatives in housing. But students who are faint of heart or afraid of things that go bump in the night ought to study the choices very carefully. After all, who wants a ghost as a roommate?

Annie at Play

One of the most magnificent buildings on the sixty-seven-acre campus of Rollins College in Winter Park is the Annie Russell Theatre. Completed in 1932, the building is of Spanish-Mediterranean Revival design, the predominant architectural style at Rollins.

Upon entering the auditorium, the first educational facility of its kind in the state, theatergoers are immediately transported to a different time and place. Its red velvet seats and hand-painted, stenciled beams hark back to the era when elegantly dressed patrons flocked to America's theaters for an evening of culture and entertainment.

There is in residence here a supernatural reminder of that golden age of the American stage. Since her death in 1936, faculty, students, and spectators alike have experienced the playful and helpful ghost of the woman for whom the theater is named.

Born in Liverpool, England, in 1869, Annie Russell came to the United States as a child. From the age of seven, the theater was Annie's home away from home. It was on the New York stage where she became an internationally renowned actress and critically acclaimed theatrical producer. In 1905, she played the title role in the stage premiere of George Bernard Shaw's *Major Barbara*. In addition to starring in more than sixty major plays, Annie produced such classics as *Much Ado About Nothing, The Rivals, She Stoops to Conquer,* and *The School for Scandal.*

In the aftermath of World War I, the celebrated actress (who was a contemporary of, but not related to, Lillian Russell) retired and moved to New Jersey. In 1923, the lure of a tropical climate led her to move to central Florida. Under her leadership and guidance, Rollins College established a dramatic-arts program. In recognition of Annie's myriad contributions to the stage and to Rollins, philanthropist Mary Curtis Bok Zimbalist funded the construction of the college's theater to honor her friend.

When the Annie Russell Theatre was dedicated on March 29, 1932, the audience thrilled to a performance of Robert Browning's *In a Balcony.* Starring in the lead role on that opening night was none other than Annie Russell.

Over the next four years, the grande dame, despite her "official" retirement, was a regular in her theater at Rollins. Whether she was working with the performing groups she founded, directing, managing, or starring in productions, or offering wisdom, inspiration, and encouragement to drama students, Annie was a fixture at the theater until her death. And so it is with her spirit!

Annie's lifelong love affair with the stage is evident in the activities of her ghost. Performers and stage personnel have come to appreciate the theatrical wraith as a protective, benevolent entity. The most superstitious of their lot believe that the ultimate success of a production depends upon whether Annie's ghost makes her appearance between midnight and one o'clock on the Wednesday morning before the opening performance. Others who are more pragmatic simply enjoy the signs of Annie's supervision: the phantom rocking chair in the prop room and the mysterious, unexplainable changes in scenery and lighting—all for the better.

On more than one occasion, the ghost has gone out of her way to look after students who share her theatrical home. Late one night, an exhausted coed fell asleep on a couch in the greenroom, only to awaken the following morning with a warm blanket covering her. A chair that had been on the other side of the room the previous evening was located adjacent to the sofa. It was as if someone had been watching over the young lady during her slumber. Subsequent inquiries revealed that no one had entered the greenroom from the time the student fell asleep until she awakened.

Had one stage worker heeded the warning of Annie's phantom touch, he might have avoided injury. Standing on a ladder, the young man was in the process of working with some lights when he felt a firm tug at the bottom of his pants. No one was nearby, so he ignored the strange pulling sensation and climbed higher. Yet it went on, as if some invisible force wanted him to come down from the ladder. Suddenly, he grabbed a live wire above him, and the electrical jolt sent his body plummeting to the floor. In an instant, colleagues rushed to his side. A desperate call was made for an ambulance, but the caller was astonished to learn that an emergency vehicle was already on its way. Had Annie summoned help?

Sometimes, would-be thespians receive Annie's approbation for their performances. At rehearsals, actors laboring to perfect their roles have been interrupted by applause coming from the otherwise empty auditorium. Innumerable performers have received a phantom pat on the back for a job well done.

No one knows exactly how or when Annie's ghost will make her next appearance. Faculty members and students familiar with her believe that the revenant uses a little-known door located on the back wall approximately fifteen feet above the stage. Various strange noises including xylophone music have been heard coming from behind the closed "Door to Nowhere," as it has been dubbed. If the door happens to be open during a stage production, theater staffers are confident that Annie is on hand.

A number of persons claim to have actually seen the ghost of Annie Russell in the building. Her apparition is said to be attired in a spectacular lavender floor-length gown of the Victorian era.

Should you have the opportunity to catch a performance in this wonderful 365-seat theater, you might want to try to obtain a seat near the aisle in the third row of the balcony. Take care not to sit in the aisle seat, which is reserved for the ghost of a very special lady. You will know her by her purple dress. If she happens to appear, mind your manners and graciously acknowledge the efforts of the performers. After all, this is her theater—the Annie Russell Theatre.

Ghostly Visages of "the Late Unpleasantness"

Few university campuses have more haunting reminders of the Civil War than Augusta State University. And for good reason. Many of the antebellum buildings on the eighty-acre main campus were constructed for the United States Arsenal, which was established here in 1827 on a site purchased from Freeman Walker, the first mayor of Augusta. When Georgia seceded from the Union in January 1861, the arsenal was sequestered by the Confederacy. It was rapidly expanded to include a massive powder works. During the four years of the maelstrom that cost more American lives than any other war, the military facilities here played a vital role in keeping the Southern war effort alive by producing upwards of thirty thousand rifle rounds per day, as well as other deadly munitions and accoutrements.

In the wake of General William T. Sherman's infamous "March to the Sea," the Confederates abandoned the Augusta complex in 1865, leaving behind the buildings and the ghosts who continue to dwell in them. Following the return of the arsenal to federal control, it remained in operation until 1955. Two years later, the Georgia State Board of Education purchased the site and converted it into the Junior College of Georgia. In 1963, the school became Augusta College upon gaining four-year status. It acquired its present name in 1996.

Today, a student body of more than five thousand men and women shares the campus with phantoms that tarry from the past. Residing in Bellevue Hall, the oldest building at Augusta State, is the most famous ghost of the university. Ever since beautiful, young Emily Galt leaped to her death from a second-story window during the Civil War, there have been reports of encounters with her abiding spirit.

By all accounts, Emily was in a state of euphoria on the eve of the conflict that would destroy her dreams and her life. Her hand was adorned with a beautiful diamond engagement ring, a gift from her handsome fiancé and a symbol of the hopes shared by the love-smitten couple. With her diamond, Emily engraved her name into a windowpane at Bellevue Hall as a lasting reminder of her bliss.

Alas, when the war began, Miss Galt's betrothed was consumed by an overwhelming sense of duty to join with his Georgia brethren in fighting for Southern independence. When he announced his fateful decision to Emily at Bellevue, a heated disagreement erupted between the two lovers. Despite the young woman's tearful protestations, her intended marched off to war.

Upon subsequent receipt of the doleful news of his death in battle, Emily Galt was overwrought with grief. Concluding that she could not live without him, she decided to join him in death.

In modern times, college officials working alone at night in Bellevue Hall have been startled to hear the arguing voices of a man and woman. Thorough searches of the building have yielded no other human presence on those occasions. At other times, the telephone system has malfunctioned without any apparent cause, and a television on the first floor has turned on and off by itself.

Many of the building's employees who have seen, heard, or otherwise experienced the strange goings-on in Bellevue consider Emily a friendly ghost. When the television suddenly comes on and tunes to NBC's *Today* show, the staff knows that Emily is up to her antics. There are, however, some employees who refuse to work in Bellevue at night for fear of witnessing hair-raising supernatural incidents, such as doors that open and close without the touch of a human hand.

Built in 1820 as a plantation house for Freeman Walker, Bellevue Hall stands at the center of the campus and serves as the university's Counseling and Testing Center. Although the window etched with Emily Galt's signature was removed during the recent renovation of the 5,026-square-foot building, the special glass has been preserved by the school.

Located next door to Bellevue Hall is the Benet House, a majestic white-columned, two-story brick structure built in 1826 as the home of the commandant of the Augusta arsenal. Subsequently, the 9,389-square-foot building was the residence of noted poet Stephen Vincent Benét. Listed on the National Register, it now houses the university's Admissions Office and several ghosts.

One of the officers who served as commandant of the arsenal was married to a vain woman of striking beauty who was in love with clothes. Her greed and all-consuming desire for the finer things in life compelled the wife to make numerous buying trips to Paris. When in residence at the Benét House, the woman would order the household servants to deliver tea to her upstairs boudoir, where she could enjoy her beverage in privacy while she admired her beautiful likeness in the mirror. Most often, she took her tea alone because her husband was either attending to his duties at the arsenal or enjoying his favorite pastime, hunting.

One morning when a maid entered the chamber of the haughty woman with a pot of tea, she was distressed to find the lady of the house cold in the grip of death. Curiously, another tray was near her lifeless body. When questioned about the matter, the commandant admitted that he had brought tea to his wife earlier in the day. Although charges were placed against him for poisoning his spouse, the officer was never convicted.

Subsequent occupants of the house have been startled by the eerie sounds of clothes swinging on the metal rod in the closet that once belonged to the commandant's wife. People familiar with the history of the house believe that the spectral sounds are made by a ghost who has a great passion for clothing.

Joining this vixenish wraith at the Benét House is the ghost of a victim of the hatred that manifested itself in the post-Civil War South. This revenant is said to be the supernatural spirit of a young Northern man whose uncle commanded the Augusta arsenal during Reconstruction.

No sooner had the fellow arrived in Augusta to work as a clerk for his uncle at an exorbitant salary of two dollars per day than the local citizenry took an intense dislike to him. Day by day, resentment grew. While at work one afternoon, the nephew made his hunger known, wondering aloud as to whether there might be some apple pie at home. As he made his way up the front steps of the Benét House, an unidentified, hidden gunman took aim and fired a bullet that killed the young man instantly. He was buried on the front lawn of the house. A tombstone with the inscription "Killed by a cowardly assassin" was placed at the grave.

Apparently, the assassin's bullet did not end the unfortunate man's quest for apple pie. To this day, occupants of the Benét House hear phantom footsteps approaching the front entrance to the house. At all hours of the day and night, the doors to the refrigerator and cabinets open and close by themselves. Drawers do likewise. The spectral search for the elusive piece of pie continues.

Located at the northwestern corner of the campus, the Walker Cemetery and the adjoining Arsenal Cemetery are the sites of supernatural activities. When Mayor Walker sold his beloved Bellevue and the adjacent seventy-two acres to the federal government, he stipulated that one acre of the arsenal property would be reserved as a cemetery for his family. An additional acre was set aside by the government as an arsenal cemetery.

Numerous ancient graves, including those of Freeman Walker and some Confederate soldiers, can be found in the cemeteries. In recent years, many reliable people, including a professor at Augusta State, have witnessed a ghostly figure attired in a gray Confederate officer's frock coat make his way from the campus to the graveyards. At the burial ground, he walks past the plots and suddenly vanishes. Visitors to the cemeteries have experienced definite cold spots while standing among the graves.

Who or what this out-of-time, out-of-place supernatural soldier is, no one knows. Maybe he is a lingering spirit from the Confederacy intent on paying his respects to his fallen comrades. Perhaps, like the other sad ghosts of Augusta State University, he lingers here as a melancholy reminder of the time when this place witnessed the ebb and flow of the fortunes of the Confederate States of America.

Scary Berry

Located on twenty-eight thousand forested acres in the mountains of northwestern Georgia, Berry College thrives as a living memorial to Martha M. Berry (1866-1942), its founder. Born into a wealthy family in nearby Rome, Georgia, Martha Berry grew up to become one of the leading educators in the United States. Her dedicated efforts to provide educational opportunities for mountain children culminated in the establishment of Berry College in 1926. She died sixteen years later, but college officials, alumni, and students alike acknowledge that her vision and her indefatigable spirit continue to be an inspiration.

And anybody familiar with the Berry College landscape knows that there are other spirits at work here as well.

Geographically, Berry is split between two campuses—the Main

Campus and the Mountain Campus. Both have a variety of ghosts. And the road connecting them—known as Stretch Road—is also haunted.

On a tour of the Main Campus, you will be hard pressed to find a building that does not have some sort of supernatural presence associated with it.

In the Ford Building complex (made possible through the generosity of automobile tycoon Henry Ford), the ghost of a female student roams the Oxford-style structures. According to reports, the student hanged herself after learning that her boyfriend had been killed in World War II.

Several spooks, all of unknown origin, inhabit nearby Blackstone Hall, constructed around 1915 as the first permanent building at Berry. All of the spectral sightings, including that of "Sepia Boy," have occurred after Blackstone was extensively renovated in 1982 to serve as the college's theater.

Morton-Lemley Hall, a dormitory for women, is haunted by Ruth, the ghost of the lady who served as a housemother back when the residence hall was occupied by male students.

Constructed in 1905, the two-story, white frame Hoge Building holds the office once used by Martha Berry. Spectral shadows and unexplainable cold spots have been encountered in her former office. A glowing yellow light has been observed coming from the building when it was otherwise dark. Hoge's ghosts are believed to be the abiding spirits of a Berry president and a professor.

Oak Hill, the stately Colonial Revival home of Martha Berry, is the most well-known haunted building on the Main Campus. Since 1972, the elegant six-columned mansion has been open to the public as a museum and visitor reception center. The student guides who lead visitors through the house have witnessed countless supernatural occurrences in the course of their duties. When tours begin each day, guides and staff members are perplexed as to how objects were moved overnight, though the house was devoid of human occupants. Nothing ever seems to vanish. Things just seem to move on their own.

Although no one has ever sighted the ghost of a child in the mansion, there is reason to believe that one is at work. Some of the items most often mysteriously displaced are the little dolls in the nursery. And from the second-floor landing, a supernatural prankster enjoys dropping or throwing small objects on or at people walking below. Often, the spook's "ammunition" takes the form of the small blue beads attached to the fringe of the curtains in an upstairs bedroom.

One ghost has been seen on occasion at Oak Hill. Known as "the White Lady," the apparition is believed to be that of Frances Rhea Berry, the sister of Martha Berry. Attired in a white dress from an earlier time, the wraith has most often been spotted on the staircase or in the bedroom that belonged to the sister.

Even when Frances Berry's ghost is not seen, its presence is felt and heard, quite frequently in the haunted bedroom. Many visitors find the room unusually cool, but that is intentional in order to protect the artifacts from humidity. Yet on occasion, some here have felt an invisible force brush against their arms, then heard the slam of the nearby bathroom door. Others have seen the doorknob of the unoccupied bathroom shake and rattle.

Stretch Road, the supernatural connector between the two haunted campuses, is the home of the Green Lady. On a dark, rainy night in the mid-1980s, a Berry coed was driving to the Mountain Campus along the lonely road when she noticed what appeared to be a small patch of fog hovering above the roadside creek. As her vehicle drew nearer, the misty spot took on a green color and formed the faint shape of a girl or young woman. The student was terrified by the spectre, which was of slender build and was attired in a tattered dress and bonnet similar to those worn in the early twentieth century—and had no eyes! After watching the thing float about a foot off the road for a few seconds, the mortified driver sped away.

Many Berry students have witnessed the same green entity while traversing Stretch Road. Some have noticed eerie green lights in their rearview mirrors, while others have driven straight through the glowing green mist that suddenly appears in the middle of the road.

Who or what the green spectre is, no one is exactly sure. Of the many explanations offered for the roadside haint, two are the most plausible. One holds that the Green Lady is the ghost of a girl who drowned in the 1930s in the creek that meanders alongside the road. Through research in the county records, and with the assistance of a Ouija board, several Berry students developed a credible alternate theory. When the students asked the board the name of the Green Lady, its answer was *Becky Stanson*. When they inquired about her year of death, the response was *1921*. As to the cause of death, the board revealed *Red Death*. Their curiosity aroused, the students traveled to the Floyd County Records Center the following day, where they made a rather remarkable discovery: a thirteen-year-old girl with a name almost identical to the one provided by the Ouija board had died in a local house fire in the early 1920s.

If the haunts of the Main Campus and Stretch Road are not scary enough for you, the ghosts of the Mountain Campus await at the end of the road. Paranormal forces have been experienced at the Hill Dining Hall, Pilgrim Hall, the Old Pig Farm, and the Dairy Barn. But the most famous haunted site here is the House of Dreams. Constructed in 1926 by the students and staff of the college as a surprise gift for Martha Berry, the expansive stone and board-and-batten cottage stands atop Lavender Mountain at an altitude of 1,360 feet.

Now used by the college for planning sessions and retreats, the House of Dreams has one permanent resident: a ghost thought to be the spirit of a woman who died tragically on the mountain. Her apparition was first observed by a Berry student who was working as an assistant to the cottage's caretaker during summer vacation.

One night, the young man crawled into his sleeping bag in the large open area on the first floor of the house. It was his lot to sleep in the place alone. In the coal-black darkness of the mountain night, the student was overcome with the fear that something was watching him. To make matters worse, he suddenly heard a loud noise in another part of the house. Leaving the warmth and relative safety of his bedding, he checked the locks on the windows and rooms of the first floor to assure himself that his mind was only playing games. But when the unnerved fellow happened to look up the stairway leading to the second story, he saw the hazy form of a woman. Clad in contemporary clothing, the apparition was that of an attractive lady in her fifties.

For some reason, the ghost seemed to be as startled as the young man. She abruptly turned and moved her hand toward her face. Then she exhibited a broad, gummy smile. It was all too apparent that the wraith had no teeth. When the student unleashed a scream, the ghost vanished and did not reappear that night, much to his relief.

Sometime later, the student was working with the caretaker in the cottage's greenhouse when the man told him about an airplane that had crashed on Lavender Mountain the previous year. Because his listener was intrigued by the story, the caretaker escorted him to the crash site. En route, the man noted that he was the one who had discovered the mangled corpses of the pilot and his wife. He noted that the bodies were "blown apart." Then he added, "I don't think we ever did get all the pieces up."

Once they reached the site of the disaster, the two men began casually looking around. Suddenly, the student noticed something embedded in the ground. Upon seeing the piece of dental work that the student had unearthed, the caretaker quipped rather matter-of-factly, "Yep, poor wife lost her dentures."

No matter which spook you happen to encounter at Berry College—the White Lady, the Green Lady, the toothless ghost, or any of the others—you will be convinced that the school richly deserves the nickname "Scary Berry."

Haunted Tales of Two Campuses

Emory University, a research institution of international renown, boasts two separate and distinct campuses. Its primary campus is located in the tree-lined suburban neighborhood of Druid Hills, some fifteen miles from downtown Atlanta. Although smaller in size, the Oxford campus, located thirty-eight miles east of Atlanta, is much older. Both sites have hauntings related to their common, yet disparate, pasts.

Chartered by the Methodist Church in 1836, Emory College took root two years later in northeastern Georgia on "virgin soil, in the midst of wide-spread and luxuriant forest of native oaks," according to Alexander Means, a professor and subsequent president of the school.

On the eve of the Civil War, the Oxford campus boasted a small assemblage of handsome structures. Today, two of those buildings are haunted by ghosts from Emory's early years.

Located at 1008 North Emory Street in Oxford, Orna Villa, a beautiful four-columned, two-story mansion, was the home of Dr. Alexander Means during his tenure as president of the school from 1854 to 1861. The dwelling is now privately owned.

Several ghosts from his time in residence still roam the place. One of the spooks is said to be Dr. Means himself.

A Methodist minister and a largely self-taught chemist and physician, Means was a scientific genius. His unique theories about electricity were so far ahead of his time that he supposedly invented and demonstrated an incandescent light in 1852, when Thomas Alva Edison was but five years old. Describing electricity as "God's vicegerent on earth," he boldly and accurately predicted that it would revolutionize the world.

Although his first love was teaching, Means agreed to serve as president of the campus at Oxford as the dark clouds of war began to envelop the South. After a day at the college, he could often be observed reading late into the night in his rocking chair at Orna Villa. At the precise moment when Dr. Means began to feel sleepy, he would begin to rock vigorously to put an end to his drowsiness. To this day, every subsequent resident of the house has reported the steady, rhythmic motion of a phantom rocking chair there. Apparently, Dr. Means is still at his reading.

Other supernatural occurrences at Orna Villa since Dr. Means's residency lend credence to the belief that the ghosts of his two sons also linger about the dwelling. Doors open and then slam shut without the aid of a human hand. Four lithographs securely attached to the interior walls have abruptly fallen to the floor simultaneously. And disembodied footsteps are heard on the front porch.

Two brothers could not have been more dissimilar in personality and preferences than Tobe and Olin Means.

Like his father, Olin valued education, so he embarked upon a medical career. While pursuing his studies, he was overwhelmed by a call to become a Methodist minister. As he wrestled to arrive at a decision, Olin was often observed walking to and fro on the front porch of Orna Villa. The phantom footsteps still heard there are said to belong to his ghost.

Tobe's ghost is believed to be the source of the other paranormal activities in the house. Contrary to the deeply held convictions of his father and brother, Tobe was of the opinion that formal education was of little benefit. He ranted and raved at his father about the money that Dr. Means had set aside for his college education. Tobe insisted that he be allowed to use it for a trip to Europe, where he would gain a more informal education. During his violent outbursts at Orna Villa, doors were slammed and pictures fell from the walls. His ghost frequently exhibits the same temperament.

Dr. Means was a delegate to the Georgia Secession Convention in January 1861. His was the voice of moderation in the early stages of the convention, but the pro-secessionists won the day, and Means ultimately voted with them. By April of the same year, the Confederate flag was hoisted at Emory College, and its students rallied around that banner. Six months later, the school closed for the duration of the war. Three of its alumni would become Confederate generals, and sixty-five Emory men would die fighting for the South.

During the four-year period of bloodshed unparalleled in American history, the campus buildings at Oxford were used as hospital facilities by both armies. Without question, the most prominent of those buildings is Phi Gamma Hall, which survives as the oldest structure on the campus. During the horrific Battle of Atlanta, Confederate forces used the stately edifice to treat the wounded and comfort the dying. Soldiers who perished in the makeshift hospital were buried in a nearby lot. Somehow, their spirits never left Phi Gamma Hall.

Constructed in 1851, the Greek Revival building now houses the campus theater. Its interior proportions are little changed from the time when the ghosts of the slain Confederate soldiers took up residence in the hall. And those ghosts are still at work. When there is no current in the wires, lights in the building turn on and off at will. Floors creak from footsteps when no human is walking upon them.

In recent years, a student was busy repairing a plaster wall in the venerable structure. To his astonishment, one small portion of the wall began to drip as the plaster dried, leaving behind the likeness of a skull.

During World War I, the Methodist Church decided to build another campus for Emory nearer to Atlanta. When the new site opened in 1919, the Oxford campus ceased to function as a college for a brief period. Now, the first two years of the liberal-arts program at Emory can be pursued at either the Oxford campus or the Atlanta campus.

The oldest building on the Atlanta campus is the Uppergate House. It is also the most haunted. Arthur Tufts, the man selected to build Emory in Atlanta, erected the three-story Italianate house as his private residence in 1916. At the age of forty, Tufts, who was also the chief of construction for the Atlanta-based Coca-Cola Company, died of influenza in the tower surmounting the second-floor bedrooms of Uppergate. Thereafter, the structure was acquired by the university.

From 1965 until 1994, Emory's Information Technology Division used the house for offices and workshops. It was during that period when the haunt first manifested itself. On a cold winter night in 1971, Mike Wilhoit, then the director of the division, halted his work on a circuit in the basement and made his way upstairs to the main computer room. En route, he unlocked the doors to the outside. As he turned a hallway corner, he was so frightened by what he encountered that he would never again work alone after dark in Uppergate.

His legs were little more than jelly after he literally bumped into her—or it. Silhouetted against the red exit light was the spectral form of a woman who stood five-foot-four. She wore a scarf on her heard. And then she spoke! Very calmly and matter-of-factly, she asked the spooked man if her son were around. Then she was gone.

Several years passed without further incident. Then Wilhoit happened to overhear a conversation among some university maintenance workers who were swapping tales about Uppergate House. He shared his ghost story about the phantom lady he had seen and heard. His listeners were not shocked at his revelation. They informed him that the spectre was the ghost of Uppergate. According to the men, the lady's son fell down the winding stairwell when the house served as a residence hall. He died from a broken neck, and since that day, his mother—or rather her spirit—has returned from time to time to look for her son.

Although Wilhoit never again experienced the presence of the Uppergate ghost, a supernatural investigation was conducted at the house with the permission of the university in 1998. Two "hot spots" of paranormal activity were located: the very place where Wilhoit's creepy encounter took place and the area at the bottom of the steep, winding front stairs. One of the investigators detected the distinct sounds of a woman singing. No other humans were about at the time, and there was no radio playing.

There are other explanations for the revenant of Uppergate.

When the house was purchased by the university in 1943, it was remodeled and used as a dormitory for student nurses. At that time, each student wore a nursing headdress similar to that sported by the ghost witnessed by Wilhoit. Maybe the apparition was that of a young student who once lived here.

And the female wraith could be that of the mother of Arthur Tufts. Records indicate that she died when Tufts was a child. Given that the contractor perished at an early age, the spectre could be a matronly spirit looking for her boy in his former home.

Prestigious Emory University offers a choice of campuses for students and visitors alike. Both at Oxford and Atlanta, Emory's storied academic history abounds. And so do its ghosts.

Three Centuries of Haunts

While meeting in Savannah on January 27, 1785, the Georgia legislature approved a charter for America's first state-supported school of higher learning, thus making the University of Georgia the oldest public university in the United States, at least on paper. It was sixteen years later when the university actually opened its doors at its present 633-acre site on the banks of the Oconee River in northeastern Georgia. History abounds on the picturesque campus, where students have studied for more than two hundred years. Not surprisingly, so do a number of ghosts representing virtually every period of the university's long and storied past.

Our visit to the historic haunted campus begins at Waddel Hall, the only early building at the University of Georgia to maintain its complete original structure. Completed in 1821, the two-story Greek Revival brick edifice was originally known as Philosophical Hall. It currently houses the Rusk Center for International Law and a ghost from the World War I era.

Expecting a joyful reunion with the love of his life after the triumphant end of the hostilities in Europe, a young soldier came home to Athens only to learn that his best girl had fallen for another. A close personal friend who lived in Waddel—which at the time served as a dormitory—allowed the soldier to use his room to discuss the delicate matter with the woman. When the couple met in Waddel, the young man's entreaties toward reconciliation were rejected, and the discussion between the two deteriorated into a bitter argument. Suddenly, the sound of loud voices gave way to two gunshots. Inside the room, authorities found the lifeless bodies of the former lovers and a suicide note. It had been penned by the heartbroken soldier, who had killed the woman and then himself. To this day, the eerie sounds of that terrible tragedy are heard by those who visit Waddel Hall.

Much like Waddel, the Lustrat House has been used by the university for many purposes. Completed in 1847, the two-story brick structure currently houses the school's Legal Affairs Department, but it was constructed as a residence for professors. And it is the ghost of a professor that continues to haunt the place.

After serving as an officer in the Confederate army, Dr. Charles Morris settled in Athens to teach at the university. For a number of years, Morris chaired the English Department, and he and his family lived in what subsequently became known as the Lustrat House. In 1903, the dwelling was moved to its present location over the vehement objections of the professor. So embittered by the relocation of his house was Dr. Morris that he refused to move with it. Later, however, his ghost moved in.

Professor Joseph Lustrat and his family took up residence in the dwelling at its current location in 1904. Over the course of their twenty-three-year residence in the house that now bears the family name, the Lustrats discovered that they shared their dwelling with a ghost. Mrs. Marie Lustrat first noticed the apparition of Dr. Morris seated at a desk near a dining-room window. Then other family members began to notice his spirit sitting in his favorite rocking chair near the fireplace in the front room. For many years, visitors to the house have been shocked to see the ghost of old Dr. Morris float down the staircase to take his favorite seat. Most often, the spectre is dressed in either a flowery nightshirt or a Confederate uniform.

Located not far from the Lustrat House is a marker for a historic oak tree that once stood in the shadow of Demosthenian Hall, the fourth-oldest building on the Athens campus. Both the marker and the two-story hall are inalterably linked to the life and times of Robert Toombs, a noted nineteenth-century statesman and soldier. Now, they are linked to his ghost.

Born in 1810 in Wilkes County, Georgia, Toombs attended Franklin College (as the University of Georgia was originally known) as a young man. School officials dismissed him because of boisterous behavior, but Toombs returned to the campus on the next commencement day and proceeded to deliver a most eloquent speech under the sweeping limbs of the massive oak that stood here. So brilliant and remarkable was his oratory that the audience assembled in Demosthenian Hall for graduation ceremonies abruptly left the building to listen to the spellbinding Toombs.

Following that dramatic presentation, Toombs went on to become one of the most renowned men in nineteenth-century Georgia. From 1852 until Georgia seceded from the Union in 1861, he served in the United States Senate. After the war began in earnest, his brief stint as secretary of state of Georgia ended when the Confederacy commissioned him a brigadier general. He served in that capacity through the Antietam campaign. When a promotion did not seem to be forthcoming, the firebrand resigned from the army.

Toombs is said to have coveted the position of Jefferson Davis, his former Senate colleague, as president of the Confederate States of

America. When the war ended, Toombs fled to Europe. In 1867, his native state welcomed the unresconstructed hero home, where he remained a political kingpin until his death.

Legend holds that when Toombs died on December 15, 1885, lightning struck and killed the majestic oak in Athens under which he began his rise to prominence. It was taken down in 1908. Much of the stump was used to fashion a lectern and platform, from which "stump" speeches are still delivered in the second-floor chamber of Demosthenian Hall. On hand to listen to the modern oratory is the ghost of Robert Toombs.

Members of the Demosthenian Society often experience Toombs's spirit while they are at work or play in the building, which was constructed in 1824. In the first-floor library, students hear footsteps in the chamber above when no one is on the second floor. The sound of boots descending the steps from the unoccupied second story has caused more than one person to inspect the staircase, only to find no one present. Lampshades spin on their own, and doors open and close at will.

On one occasion, several students were playing cards on the first floor when they were overcome by the distinct feeling that there was an unseen presence in the room. Momentarily putting aside their cards, the young men were startled to see someone peek around the corner. A search revealed no other human presence in the building.

Passersby have heard speeches coming from the venerable building when it was empty. Others have seen a pale white face peering out of a window of the hall when it was unoccupied.

Several campus office buildings have spooks of more recent origin. Employees in the Business Services Building have been mystified by the unearthly moans and other creepy noises coming from the basement of the structure. Those eerie sounds were routinely attributed to the settling of the building until workers learned that the basement was once used as the embalming room of the mortuary in the former Bernstein Building.

Joe Brown Hall is haunted by the ghost of a student who accidentally killed himself at a time when the two-story building served as a residence hall. Because he died during a school break, a period of time passed before his decomposing corpse was discovered. Subsequently, building residents complained of a smell of death that could not be removed. Strange, unexplainable sights and sounds began to frighten students. Bloodstains from the tragedy were carefully cleaned and removed, but they returned time and time again.

In time, university officials decided to remodel Joe Brown Hall and convert it to office use. A stairway said to lead to the room once occupied by the unfortunate boy was blocked off. It now leads to a dead end much like the ones found in the famed Winchester Mystery House in California. Nonetheless, professors and students have detected bizarre knocking sounds coming from the sealed room. Some custodians have refused to work in the building after the sun goes down. They have reported feeling unusual cold spots in the stairway to nowhere and seeing the apparition of a young man staring at them.

A significant number of Greek houses at the university have ghosts. At the Phi Kappa Psi house, the brothers share their place with the ghost of a crying baby. Formerly used as Athens General Hospital, the Zeta Beta Phi house is inhabited by the wraith of a girl who died in a mysterious accident at the hospital. Members of the Sigma Nu fraternity live with the ghost of William Simpson, a brother who fell to his death from a second-story window in the 1950s. Sisters living at the Phi Mu house are haunted by the ghosts of a couple whose tryst ended in tragedy before the dwelling was converted into a sorority house.

Perhaps the most haunted Greek house at the University of Georgia is the Alpha Gamma Delta house at 530 South Milledge Avenue. W. W. Thomas constructed the impressive house as a marriage gift for his daughter, Susie, in the last decade of the nineteenth century. The home actually resembles a wedding cake.

On the afternoon set aside for the nuptials, friends and family gathered at the house for the ceremony. Alas, when the appointed hour came, the groom was nowhere to be found. Ten minutes passed, then twenty. As the frustrated parents of the bride attempted to dissuade guests from leaving, the distraught Susie slipped away from the crowd and made her way up to the room on the upper right side of the dwelling. There, she hanged herself.

Amid all the confusion downstairs, Susie's parents grew concerned about her absence. They walked upstairs to discover the hideous sight of the dangling body. At about the same time, the tardy groom arrived. En route to the ceremony, his carriage had overturned.

Somehow, Susie's spirit must have learned that her fiancé had been true, because her wedding house has been just that since the sorority purchased it in 1939. The room in which Susie died is known as "the Engagement Suite," because every sister who has occupied it has become pinned or engaged while living in the room.

And there is more. A painting of the house that has long adorned the walls of the sorority shows a beam of light streaming from the heavens to the special room. The artist maintains that he did not include the stream of light in his work.

Around for much of the American national experience, the University of Georgia has established itself as one of the South's most respected public universities. All the while, its ghosts have worked hard to establish the school as one of Dixie's most haunted.

A Curse on Transylvania

By logic, a supernatural tale about a university by the name of Transylvania should involve a bloodthirsty vampire in the Carpathian Mountains of Romania. Logic aside, our tale is set in Lexington, Kentucky, at America's oldest university west of the Allegheny Mountains. And rather than the fictional creature of the night made famous by author Bram Stoker and the moviemaking magic of Hollywood, it is Constantine Rafinesque (1783-1840), a brilliant, rather eccentric French scientist—or at least his curse—that haunts Transylvania University to this very day.

"Transy," as the university is known to students and supporters, is a small, private liberal-arts school of about eleven hundred students. Founded in 1780, the university is the twelfth-oldest institution of higher learning in the United States and boasts a proud heritage. Its Latin name, which translates as "across the woods," was given to the vast frontier region in Kentucky to which some enterprising North Carolina businessmen dispatched the intrepid explorer Daniel Boone in the eighteenth century.

Constantine Rafinesque, who has been called "the Daniel Boone of American science," arrived at Transylvania in 1819 to serve as professor of modern languages and natural history. By that time, the university had already established itself as one of the preeminent seats of learning in the United States. A number of America's founding fathers, including George Washington, John Adams, Aaron Burr, and Thomas Jefferson, supported and praised Transylvania, whose medical and law schools were among the first in the new country. Jefferson, the father of the University of Virginia, expressed his envy of Transylvania at about the time Rafinesque joined its faculty: "We must send our children for education to Kentucky [Transylvania] or to Cambridge [Harvard]. . . . If we are to go begging anywhere for an education, I would rather it should go to Kentucky because she has more the flavor of the old cask than any other."

The list of early graduates of Transylvania yields a glimpse of the fame enjoyed by the university: Stephen Austin, Cassius M. Clay, Jefferson Davis, two vice presidents of the United States, fifty United States senators, 101 United States representatives, two United States Supreme Court justices, and thirty-six governors. Among its early faculty members and trustees was the famous statesman Henry Clay.

Indeed, Constantine Rafinesque came to Transylvania at a time when the university's prestige was great and its future bright. But the days of glory were fleeting. Today, the school rests quietly on a six-block campus in the heart of Lexington. What happened? Many believe that Transylvania's decline in prominence is directly related to the words uttered by Rafinesque when he departed the campus in disgust in 1826: "Damn thee and thy school as I place a curse upon you."

Constantine Samuel Rafinesque was born October 22, 1783, in Constantinople to a French father and a German mother. His father moved the family to Marseilles, France, when Rafinesque was but an infant, and it was there that the child lived until the French Revolution. In 1802, Rafinesque and his brother were sent to America by their family to avoid the military and political turmoil in Europe.

Following in his father's footsteps as a merchant, Rafinesque attained a measure of affluence in Philadelphia. His wealth enabled him to pursue his true passion: natural history. Traveling throughout eastern America and portions of Europe during the first two decades of the nineteenth century, Rafinesque established himself as a pioneer in the scientific study of American natural history.

Thomas Jefferson offered to appoint Rafinesque as the official botanist of the famed Lewis and Clark expedition, but the scientist disdained the offer, choosing instead to pursue his independent studies. In his quest for knowledge, he walked some twenty-six thousand miles through much of the American frontier to obtain samples of the unnamed and uncataloged flora and fauna. On his expeditions, he refused to ride a horse, saying that it was too much trouble to dismount to obtain specimens.

Why Rafinesque chose to settle in Kentucky remains a subject of debate. Some historians believe that he came to work with his famed peer John James Audubon. An eight-day sojourn at Audubon's Kentucky estate in 1819 did not go well. Egos clashed, and Rafinesque's discovery of a previously unclassified species of bat in Audubon's house did little to foster cooperation. After bidding adieu, Rafinesque accepted an offer from John D. Clifford, a former business associate who had become a trustee at Transylvania, to teach at the school.

When he joined the distinguished faculty, Rafinesque was a well-known scholar. His seven-year tenure at Transylvania allowed him to produce some of his best work as a natural scientist, historian, and author. However, his service at the university was not without almost constant controversy. His enthusiasm for scientific discovery caused the professor to miss more classes than did his students. His immodest, harsh demeanor and his unkempt physical appearance made him unpopular with the faculty and the student body. His colleagues classified him as an "odd fish," and his pupils nicknamed him "the Mad Botanist." His lectures were deemed boring because Rafinesque was unable to present the material on a level his students could understand.

His eccentricity and unusual personality brought Rafinesque into conflict with Horace Holley, the president of Transylvania. Matters came to a head in 1826, when the scientist returned to the Lexington campus after one of his frequent, unannounced trips to the frontier. In his absence, Holley had sequestered the campus quarters occupied by Rafinesque and had, according to the professor, "thrown all of my effects, books and collections in a heap in another room."

Officially, Rafinesque was dismissed by Holley for "unprofessional conduct." Off the record, fingers were pointed at another person as the reason for the termination. The president suspected—apparently with good reason—that Rafinesque and Holley's wife were engaged in a romantic affair. Though the illicit relationship was never proved, Rafinesque was known to have written poetry for Mrs. Holley, and she, unlike the rest of the university community, openly displayed fondness for the professor.

When Horace Holley informed Rafinesque of his dismissal, the professor became highly incensed and pronounced the now infamous curse on the school and its president.

From Lexington, Rafinesque returned to Philadelphia, where he lived for the remainder of his life. He died of liver and stomach cancer on September 19, 1840, some eight years after he had obtained American citizenship. Because he was a virtual pauper at his death, friends provided the necessary funds for his burial.

During his lifetime, Rafinesque was accorded few of the honors and little of the recognition that were due him as one of the foremost naturalists in early American history. Many of his contemporaries attempted to discredit him by claiming that his research was sloppy. Only after his death did historians and scientists pay homage to the far-thinking little man who authored more than 220 books, essays, and other scientific treatises and left behind a theory of evolution predating that of Charles Darwin by more than twenty years.

And what about the curse he left behind?

In 1827, the year after the scientist left Transylvania in disgust, the state refused to provide any further funding for the university, thereby causing Horace Holley to resign as president. Holley promptly left Lexington and died suddenly and unexpectedly of yellow fever on July 31, 1827, while sailing to Boston. He was buried at sea.

Back in Lexington, a terrible conflagration erupted a year later in the principal campus building after a servant knocked over a burning candle. In the wake of the inferno, stunned witnesses searched the smoldering ruins. Mysteriously, the only articles not consumed by the fire were the papers and effects left behind by Rafinesque, who was in Philadelphia at the time of the fire.

Seven years after Rafinesque departed Transylvania, workmen were busy putting the finishing touches on the new campus centerpiece, a massive Greek Revival building now affectionately known as "Old Morrison." As the building neared completion, construction had to be halted for months when a terrible cholera epidemic swept through the university community.

Transylvanians who were familiar with the curse annunciated by Rafinesque began to look at the calendar. They whispered that the university was destined to suffer tragedies every seven years as a result of the bedevilment of the former professor. As time went by, their worst fears were realized. Someone associated with the university died a mysterious, violent death every seven years.

In 1924, friends and supporters of Transylvania mounted a successful fund-raising effort to exhume the grave of Rafinesque and rebury his remains in a special crypt in Old Morrison. Publicly, the project was hailed as a proper way to honor the memory of the scientist, whose plot at the Philadelphia cemetery was in such a state of disrepair that it was in danger of being lost. Privately, there was talk that the exhumation and reburial effort was initiated in an attempt to end the curse.

Actually, the remains relocated to the Lexington campus may not have been those of the scientist, since five or six additional people had been interred in his plot after his death. Regardless, a marble slab inscribed with the words "Honor to Whom Honor Is Overdue" was placed atop the tomb of Rafinesque at Transylvania.

Despite the best of intentions, the curse was not broken with the reburial. Suicides, murders, and strange fires have continued.

In the early 1960s, the lifeless body of a strangled coed was discovered in her vehicle, parked within sight of the crypt. And then, as the decade was nearing an end, a mysterious fire engulfed Old Morrison and gutted the entire building, save for one room—that housing the tomb of Constantine Rafinesque. Firefighters who battled the fire on the first level of the historic edifice witnessed a mystifying and terrifying sight as the flames made their way toward the tomb. At the door of the crypt, the fire formed a wall and spread no further. At the entrance to the tomb, the firefighters saw the spectre of a man. He offered a contemptible laugh before suddenly vanishing into the flames. Once the holocaust was extinguished, university and public-safety officials surveyed the smoking rubble. When they came upon the lone standing room, they were shocked to find Rafinesque's crypt very cold, as if there had been no fire.

Old Morrison was subsequently reconstructed, but the ancient spell has not been broken. A night watchman in the restored building sustained an injury when he tripped over a phantom object and fell in a dark hallway. No physical cause for the accident was found. Then a maintenance worker died when he mysteriously fell from the roof of the school's basketball arena.

Despite the curse that yet haunts the campus, the university pays homage to "Rafy," as the scientist is now known to students. One of the main dining facilities on campus is "the Rafskeller." During the Halloween season, Transylvania celebrates Rafinesque Week with a dance and other festivities in a good-natured attempt to honor the old professor.

Should you desire to visit Rafinesque's mysterious crypt, it is located at the heart of the ancient campus in Old Morrison. Prudent visitors will do well, however, to schedule a visit that does not coincide with a year when the curse of the Mad Botanist is at work on Transylvania.

Here, There, and Everywhere— Ghosts!

Adorning a hill some 125 feet above downtown Bowling Green, the two-hundred-acre campus of Western Kentucky University is regarded as one of the loveliest in all of America. In 1911, the school was moved to the current site. Since that time, it has continued to grow in size and beauty. A handsome assemblage of fifty-three buildings representing a variety of architectural styles now graces the verdant landscape on the commanding promontory. These structures stand as monuments to Western Kentucky's proud tradition as an institution established to educate teachers.

Roaming the hallowed halls of a number of the buildings are spectral reminders of another chapter from the school's storied history—its legendary, and often dark, supernatural past. Suicides, tragic accidents, and even murders claimed the lives of most of the individuals who abide on the hilltop campus in spirit form.

Potter Hall, one of Western's oldest buildings, was constructed as a women's dormitory in 1921. Today, it houses the ghost of a female student who took her life in her basement room on April 21, 1979. On that night, Theresa Watkins, a resident of Room 7, was so emotionally distressed that she hanged herself with a belt looped over the ceiling steam pipes. News of her suicide devastated the university community.

Not long after the gruesome incident, eerie things began to happen in Potter. Chairs and other items mysteriously moved without the aid of human hands. Coins dropped into vending machines when no person was about. Disembodied footsteps caused the floors of the lobby to creak and groan. Unable to explain the odd occurrences, students attributed the paranormal activity to Theresa Watkins's ghost.

While engrossed in serious study in their rooms at Potter, residents have been interrupted by a phantom female voice calling their names. At other times, a cold breeze has blown through rooms with closed doors. Creaky room doors have opened without human touch.

During a school break when most students were away, two campus security officers made their way to Potter one evening while on routine patrol. One of the officers began to relate the story of Theresa's ghost as they entered the building. Suddenly, they heard a banging sound that seemed to be coming from the basement. In a flash, the man and woman scrambled in the direction of the noise. Soon, they found themselves standing in front of Room 7. As the female officer searched for the key to open the locked door, the commotion continued inside the room.

In a spooked voice, the male officer asked, "Did you see that?"

His partner looked up from her ring of keys and asked, "See what?"

He directed her attention to the doorknob, which was turning as if someone had control of it on the other side. When the officers opened the door, they found nothing more than some old mattresses. The room window was locked tight.

In 1994, Potter Hall was converted into an administration building. Since that time, Theresa's presence has been documented less frequently. Nonetheless, loud banging on the pipes still comes from Room 7.

Adjacent to Potter Hall stands stately Van Meter Hall, which was completed in 1911 as the administration building and auditorium for the school. As work on the two-thousand-seat chamber was nearing an end, a construction worker was killed when he fell through a skylight and landed on the stage floor. According to reports, the laborer lost his balance after he was distracted by an airplane flying overhead—a rather curious sight in that day.

When witnesses rushed to aid the unfortunate victim, they found his lifeless body in a large pool of blood on the stage. Since the man's death, a large bloodstain has reappeared at that very spot time after time during dramatic presentations and rainstorms. Numerous efforts to rid the hall of the hideous bloodstain—including several replacements of the stage floor—have failed. Somehow, the blood continues to soak through the flooring.

Lighting malfunctions in the auditorium have also been blamed on the construction worker. On occasion during a performance, a light will mysteriously shine on the exact bloody spot where the man landed. Custodial employees often turn off lights at night only to witness them turn on again in a few seconds.

Performers have also experienced the activities of the Van Meter ghost. Props have been turned over, music stands have been rearranged, and the stage curtains have opened and closed, all without human assistance.

Some people have reported seeing the spectre of the workman in the auditorium. While dressing for a performance, more than one thespian has glanced into his mirror and noticed a man standing there. A quick glance to the rear has revealed no human presence. Described by those who have seen him as a man in his fifties, the ghost appears as a figure of white or bluish light.

One evening after Van Meter was closed and locked tight, a campus security officer sprang into action when he observed a man enter the building. In an attempt to nab the intruder, the officer hurried into Van

Meter and followed the distinct sound of footsteps down a hallway. At length, it sounded as if the trespasser had entered a room with only one door. Satisfied that he had cornered the man, the policeman carefully entered the room, where he found nothing. His bewilderment grew moments later when he heard an evil cackle outside in the hallway. Shining his flashlight up and down the corridor, the officer found no trace of a human presence.

Other mysterious sounds have been heard in Van Meter. At times, the phantom voices of a woman and a child have echoed through the auditorium. Some believe these haunting utterances are the cries of a wife and daughter seeking their family member who died here.

Located not far from Van Meter and Potter is Florence Schneider Hall, a three-story coed dormitory completed in the Georgian Revival style in 1929. Here, too, the resident ghost is associated with a terrible tragedy. A half-century ago, two female residents of Schneider decided to forego spring break in order to catch up on their studies. One of the girls, known for the purposes of this story as Janet, was working at her desk one quiet evening when an escaped mental patient burst into her room through an open window. Armed with an ax, the deranged man attacked Janet, slammed the sharp blade into her head, and vanished as quickly as he had appeared.

Mortally injured by the vicious blow, Janet somehow managed to crawl to her friend's room, located down the hall. Despite the weakness occasioned by her heavy loss of blood, the young woman, with the ax embedded in her skull, used her last bit of energy to scratch on the door in a desperate attempt to obtain help. Inside, Janet's friend was so frightened by the scratching sound that she would not open the door.

The following morning, she ventured forth to discover the hideous sight.

Since Janet's death, her ghost has made itself known in the room where she was attacked. Subsequent residents have observed her spectre sitting in the window. Others have experienced her paranormal activities: turning computers, alarm clocks, and other electronic devices on and off; moving furniture; and displacing other objects. Even more frightening are the scratching sounds that are often heard on doors along the hallway where Janet crawled on the night of her death.

Towering on the northwest side of campus not far from Schneider is Rodes-Harlin Hall. Completed in 1966, the tall brick edifice of modern design also serves as a coed dormitory. Over the years, students here have been annoyed by frequent elevator breakdowns and rodent infestations and have been terrified by the building's resident ghost.

The haunt of Rodes-Harlin is said to be the spirit of a female student who committed suicide some years ago. From the roof of the tall residence hall, the distraught student jumped to her death. Not long thereafter, her roommate began to hear an unusual tapping sound at her door. Each time she opened it, there was no one about. Every year on the anniversary of the suicide, the ghost of the young lady is observed roaming the dorm. On other days, students living on the ninth floor can hear phantom footsteps on the roof above them at the very spot from which the girl made her fatal leap.

Two campus landmarks house the ghosts of men who died as a result of elevator mishaps.

At twenty-seven stories, the Pearce-Ford Tower is the tallest building on the Western Kentucky campus. At least three ghosts are known to haunt the tallest residence hall in Kentucky.

Before it was completed in 1971, the tower was the scene of a tragedy when a construction laborer fell from the top floor down the long elevator shaft. After the building opened, residents began to notice that the elevators sometimes ran by themselves. Even now, the elevators at times move up and down at will without a human touch. Speculation is that the phantom movements are caused by the worker who descended to his death in the very shaft where the elevators now run.

On rarer occasions, the elevator doors have opened to reveal a car empty save for the ghostly construction worker.

Another ghost prowls the elevators of the Pearce-Ford Tower. It is the spirit of a former male resident who refused to shower in the bathroom on his own floor. One night, after finishing his shower on another floor, the towel-clad fellow made his way to the elevator and pushed the button. When the malfunctioning door opened, he stepped forward and plummeted twenty stories. From time to time, students see wet footprints in the empty elevator car on the floor where the student took his shower.

A third tragedy claimed the life of a worker at Pearce-Ford in the fall of 1994 when a seven-thousand-pound heating-and-cooling unit crushed the man. From that day forward, the air-conditioning system has malfunctioned and rattled at various times without rational explanation. Some of those familiar with the accident attribute the problems to the ghost of the victim.

Over at Barnes-Campbell Hall, an elevator accident in the nine-story dormitory on November 9, 1967, gave birth to the resident wraith. Although the building was less than two years old at the time, its elevators were prone to breaking down. On the day in question, James W. Duvall, a twenty-year-old resident assistant on the sixth floor, left a bathroom on the fifth floor after finishing his shower. Attired only in a robe, he walked down the hallway to the elevator. Immediately, he noticed that it was stuck on the sixth floor.

Although university officials had admonished him about acting as an amateur repairman, James had remedied the elevator problem once before with relative ease. All he had to do now was to locate the key, pry open the door, reach into the shaft, and turn the switch. After all, he did not want to take the steps to the sixth floor.

All went well until James leaned into the shaft. His wet feet caused him to slip as the car began to descend from above. He was pinned between the outer shaft and the moving elevator. It took more than an hour for emergency workers to extricate his crushed, lifeless body.

Soon after the grisly incident, the ghost of the ill-fated junior began to make its presence known. Countless students and university employees have noticed that the elevator sometimes mysteriously moves to the sixth floor when no one is using it. Often, the elevator will stop late at night on the fifth floor, and the door will open to reveal a vacant car. On occasion, the phantom resident assistant has even traced the route of his fatal trip to the elevator. When the fifth-floor hallway is devoid of human occupants, a trail of wet footprints has appeared leading from the bathroom where James showered for the last time to the elevator that cost him his life.

Resident assistants and university officials have experienced the mischievous activities of the Barnes-Campbell ghost during school breaks. During one spring vacation, two resident assistants returned from supper to find water running from every faucet on the fifth floor. One summer, Howard Bailey, the dean of student life, was assigned to monitor the vacant building while the students were away. On more than one nocturnal visit to the unoccupied building, Bailey heard metal trash cans being thrown down the stairwells. No other human was in Barnes-Campbell at the time.

Even several Greek houses at Western Kentucky have ghosts born of tragedy. A woman murdered long ago in the Tudor-style house at 1504 Chestnut Street continues to haunt the place, which is now the home of the Lambda Chi Alpha fraternity. The brothers have seen the spectral form of the woman race across the front yard. Inside the house, the phantom has started fires in the fireplace, turned lights on and off, moved objects, and activated alarm clocks in the middle of the night.

Even though the Lambda Chi Alpha ghost is something of a prankster, she has never caused harm to any residents of the house. To the contrary, she may be trying to set a good example for the men. One night, a brother was disturbed from a deep sleep by an unusual noise. He followed the sound to an empty room that was locked. Pouring from the crack under the door was an eerie glow. From the unoccupied room came the distinct sound of clicking typewriter keys. Perhaps the ghost was burning the midnight oil at her literary pursuits.

At the Sigma Alpha Epsilon house on College Street, the brothers share their dwelling with the ghost of a Civil War soldier. During the great conflict of the nineteenth century, Kentucky was a state deeply torn by divided allegiances. Many soldiers from both warring armies camped in and around the current site of the university. Battlefield casualties were brought to a hospital located in the existing chapter house. The ghost of one of those war victims apparently never left the place after the soldier expired.

Fraternity brothers past and present have witnessed the translucent silhouette of a tall, slender man attired in a Civil War-era hat and overcoat. Sometimes when the soldier's ghost is not seen, his presence is heard or felt. Without human assistance, doors open and close and appliances turn on. Frequently, the brothers hear phantom footsteps pacing to and fro over the creaky floorboards of the ancient structure.

Not every ghost at Western Kentucky is the result of a life that came to a tragic end. Located near Rodes-Harlin Hall, the Kentucky Building opened in 1939 as a repository for artifacts and historic documents relating to Kentucky and its people. Over the years, staff members and patrons have experienced many eerie things in the facility: a spectre attired in old-fashioned clothing, unexplained noises, books pulled from storage and opened to particular pages, an eerie white haze, and sudden rushes of cold air. Many employees in the building have reported the odd sensation that they were being watched by an unseen entity.

After visiting the Kentucky Building, a psychic concluded that the artifacts bear the imprints of the persons formerly associated with them. According to her theory, these imprints produce energy that manifests itself in the form of the supernatural goings-on observed in the museum/library.

McLean Hall, a dormitory located just south of Schneider Hall, was the first campus building named in honor of a woman. Mattie McLean served as secretary for Henry Hardin Cherry, the first president of the school, until his death in 1937. "Miss Mattie," as she was affectionately known, was a beloved figure at Western until she died in 1954, just three years after the residence hall was named for her. Apparently, she—or her spirit, at least—never left the campus. For years, her ghostly form has strolled the halls of her dorm, often playing tricks on the residents but always watching over them like a grand matron.

On some university campuses, one must look high and low to find a haunt in residence. But at Western Kentucky University, the school on the hilltop, ghosts abound almost everywhere.

Isabella

Tangible evidence of Louisiana's rich French heritage abounds throughout the state. Natchitoches, now a city of twenty-five thousand residents, was the oldest permanent settlement in the Louisiana Purchase. It traces its roots to a French fort built here in 1714.

Within this ancient city, Northwestern State University is located on the spacious grounds of the former Bullard Plantation. Three columns are all that remain of the four-columned Bullard Mansion, an imposing antebellum edifice that stood on the campus until it was demolished at the beginning of the twentieth century. The surviving columns endure as a romantic symbol of the university and its past. But within the shadows of the massive pillars and the darkness of the nearby campus buildings, there resides the ghost of Isabella, a young French maiden whose unhappy life ended here in the mid-nineteenth century.

In the years preceding the Civil War, Isabella, known throughout northwestern Louisiana for her stunning beauty, counted many suitors. But when a dashing young man from the East came to Natchitoches on business one day, Isabella's life was never the same. For her, it was love at first sight. A tender romance evolved between the two, and the passionate couple agreed to marry.

With each passing day as the wedding grew nearer, Isabella could hardly contain her happiness and excitement. Then, just days before the planned nuptials, the young businessman was killed in a duel. Rumor had it that the deadly clash was the culmination of a dispute over another woman.

Emotionally devastated by the loss of the love of her life, the bereaved Isabella sought seclusion. She became a nun, joining the Society of the Sacred Heart, which had established a convent at the Bullard Mansion in 1856.

At the convent, Isabella was a recluse. She spent her days and nights mourning alone in her room. On the infrequent occasions when she made her way outside the old plantation house, she could be seen walking about the convent grounds and talking to her deceased fiancé.

Her sisters in the convent grew increasingly concerned about Isabella's erratic behavior. They feared that she had gone mad.

One night, a terrific storm bore down on Natchitoches. Concerned about their safety, the nuns made their way down to the lower floor of the old mansion. But not Isabella! She locked the door of her room on the upper floor.

Throughout the night, the storm raged with great fury. When calm came in the early morning, several of the nuns went upstairs to check on Isabella. Since her door was locked, the women used force to open it. In the room, they found Isabella's body with a knife thrust through her heart. Her bloody hand print stained a wall.

Not long after Isabella's burial, her ghost began roaming the old Bullard Mansion and the plantation grounds. When the convent site was acquired by the state of Louisiana in 1885 to serve as the campus of the newly created Louisiana State Normal School, Isabella's spirit remained in residence at the mansion.

Some thought that the supernatural presence might come to an end when in 1904 the venerable structure was leveled—save three of the columns on its eastern side—to make way for the construction of East Hall. To the contrary, as soon as the new building was completed, Isabella took up residence there.

Twenty-two years later, East Hall was demolished and replaced by the Music Education Building. The students, sensing that Isabella had become a permanent resident of the school, began a campus tradition of "escorting" the ghost to the new structure erected at the site of the former convent.

In 1944, the state legislature changed the name of the school to Northwestern State University, which today boasts a student body of more than six thousand men and women at the Natchitoches campus.

When the Music Education Building was razed after World War II, a group of spirited male students donned white sheets and attempted to lure Isabella's ghost from the building. For the next three years, it seemed that Isabella had no home, for she was observed flitting from building to building near "the Columns."

According to campus tradition, Isabella chose Caldwell Hall as her new home on January 15, 1949. Newspaper accounts reported that a letter from the ghost and a few drops of blood were found on the steps of the building on that night.

A mysterious fire destroyed Caldwell in 1982, thus depriving Isabella of her home once again. Later that year, a campus event on Halloween night attracted national press coverage, when Isabella was ceremoniously moved to vacant Nelson Hall, the former gymnasium for women, built around 1923. Because of its proximity to the old mansion site, Nelson proved to be a suitable home for the ghost. For almost twenty years, Isabella had the building to herself.

On Halloween night in 2001, the university conducted a special ceremony to welcome Isabella to the fully renovated Nelson Hall, which now houses the National Center for Preservation Technology and Training, a division of the National Park Service.

Whether or not Isabella is happy with the changes made to her newest home remains to be determined. In each of the previous buildings she has inhabited, her bloody hand print has been observed. Perhaps that was her ghostly seal of approval at each place.

One thing appears to be certain: Isabella's ghost intends to remain very close to the place where the heartbroken young lady lived her last days. From time to time, every building near the three columns has experienced her supernatural presence. Take, for example, Varnado Hall. In the foyer that divides the east and west halls of the dormitory, melancholy piano music has been heard on many occasions when no one was at the piano.

A tour of the beautiful thousand-acre campus of Northwestern State University is highly recommended. Not to be missed is the old quadrangle where the Bullard Mansion once stood. In 1980, this area was listed on the National Register of Historic Places.

Should you happen to visit the site on a stormy night and hear a doleful wail, it might be just the wind, or it could be the cry of the legendary *loup-garou*—or werewolf—said to inhabit the bayous of Louisiana. But most likely, you will have heard the siren call of the ghost of a French beauty named Isabella, who yet weeps for a love who died so long, long ago.

The Miracle at Grand Coteau

Located on the Zydeco-Cajun Prairie Byway in southwestern Louisiana, where Creole and Cajun French are still spoken, Grand Coteau has long been recognized as one of the most important early centers of Roman Catholic education west of the Mississippi. A state historical marker in the town pays homage to its two most venerable institutions: the Academy of the Sacred Heart, established in 1821 as the second-oldest institution of learning in the western United States, and Saint Charles Borromeo College, established in 1838 by French Jesuit priests as the first Catholic school for males in Louisiana. In the twentieth century, the college closed its doors to lay students, but it continues to function as a Jesuit seminary today.

In the second half of the nineteenth century, the Academy of the Sacred Heart achieved enduring fame as the site of the only miracle recognized by the Roman Catholic Church to have taken place in the United

States. A phantom priest who now walks the halls of nearby Saint Charles Borromeo College may be the apparition of the man whose intercession produced the miracle.

Mary Wilson, the recipient of the miracle, was born in Canada on September 20, 1846. She journeyed to St. Louis, Missouri, at the age of sixteen. There, Mary, reared a Presbyterian, joined the Roman Catholic Church. At the age of twenty, she decided to become a nun. Despite her youth, Mary's health was not good, so the Sisters of the Sacred Heart sent her to Grand Coteau, where she could complete her training in a more favorable climate.

In October 1866, just a month after her arrival at the academy, Mary was hospitalized in the infirmary when her medical condition worsened. She described her problems thusly: "On the 19th day of October, I was obligated to repair to the infirmary, and I did not leave it until the 17th day of December. During all this time I was dangerously ill, vomiting blood two and three times a day, with constant fever and violent headaches the greater part of the time."

Despite a lack of appetite, Mary attempted to eat at the insistence of her physicians, but her intake of food brought on severe spasms. On November 7, extreme unction (last rites) was administered to the ailing young woman. Over the next month, Mary noted, "my sufferings were so intolerable that it seemed to me that it was impossible to bear them long."

Their faith ever strong, the sisters at the academy commenced a novena to John Berchmans, whereby they prayed that God would cure or provide relief to Mary through the intercession of Berchmans. Just a year earlier, Pope Pius XI had approved the beatification of Berchmans, which was the first step on the road to sainthood. Born March 15, 1599, in Diest, Belgium, Berchmans aspired to be a Jesuit priest but died before he could complete his studies and take his vows of ordination.

Despite the novena, Mary's condition further deteriorated. She later recalled, "The third day of my novena, my illness seemed to assume a more alarming aspect, and for five days, I suffered intensely. During the last three, especially, I endured the pangs of death. My body was drawn up with pain, my hands and feet were cramped and cold in death. All of my sickness had turned to inflammation of the stomach and throat. My tongue was raw and swollen. I was not able to speak for two days. At each attempt to utter a word, the blood would gush from my mouth."

For some forty days, the suffering young woman had been unable to eat solid food. For two weeks, she had received no medication because the attending physician believed it was useless to torture her any longer.

On Friday morning, December 17, a priest came to Mary to administer Holy Communion in viaticum, given to those in imminent danger of dying. He told her that very soon she would "enter upon the long voyage of eternity."

In the hours that followed, Mary, who could no longer speak, waited with her eyes closed for death to come. Suddenly, she heard a whisper: "Open your mouth." Responding as best she could, she experienced relief when someone put a finger on her tongue. Then she heard the voice again, this time in a loud, more distinct tone: "Sister, you will get the desired habit. Be faithful. Have confidence. Fear not."

Mary had not opened her eyes and thus did not see who was ministering to her. In an excited voice, she exclaimed, "But Mother Moran, I am well!"

When Mary looked up from her bed, she beheld a figure holding a cup in his hands. Light was about his countenance. Taken aback by what she saw, the startled young lady shut her eyes and queried, "Is it Blessed Berchmans?"

The answer was that which she expected: "Yes, I come by the order of God. Your sufferings are over. Fear not."

When Mary once again opened her eyes, the figure was gone.

Presently, the sister infirmarian returned to the room from the chapel, only to be greeted by the patient, who announced with happiness, "It is true. Blessed Berchmans has cured me!"

No one was more astonished by Mary's miraculous recovery than her physician. After a complete examination of her mouth and tongue, he proclaimed that "no human means could have produced such an effect."

On the following Monday, Mary's dearest hopes were realized when she received the holy habit of the Order of the Sacred Heart. Though her recovery was complete, she would not live long enough to learn that the intercession on her behalf would be recognized as an authentic miracle.

The spirit of John Berchmans visited the young woman once more, on January 27, 1867. Less than eight months later, she died following a "cerebral attack."

Prior to Mary's death, however, documentation had already been forwarded to the archbishop of New Orleans to begin the process of recognition of the healing at Grand Coteau as a miracle. Among the paperwork was a statement by Dr. William Millard that read, "Not being able to discover any marks or convalescence; but an immediate return to health from a severe and painful illness, I am unable to explain the transition by any ordinary natural laws."

In 1888, Pope Leo XIII canonized John Berchmans as a saint of the Roman Catholic Church and recognized the healing of Mary Wilson as a miracle. To memorialize the place where the miracle of Grand Coteau occurred, the academy converted the infirmary into a chapel and erected a shrine to Saint John Berchmans in the same second-floor room where he appeared to Mary Wilson.

Today, a beautiful avenue of ancient oak trees extends from the front gate of the academy to the town of Grand Coteau. The trees were planted in the nineteenth century to protect priests from the sun as they rode on horseback between Saint Charles Borromeo College and the academy. Now, each summer, this arbor alleyway welcomes visitors who want to see Saint Charles Borromeo, the famous Roman Catholic educational complex. Jesuit priests still come and go there as they have for generations. But one of their number always appears in spectral form. Could it be the abiding spiritual presence of the man who gained sainthood because of his intercession here in the days following the Civil War?

Mary of Callaway

Columbus, the home of Mississippi University for Women, is a very historic and haunted city. Located on the Tombigbee River in east-central Mississippi just south of the Alabama border, Columbus served as the state capital during the Civil War. Of the numerous majestic antebellum mansions in and around the city, at least five are inhabited by ghosts. And so, too, is its university.

Known to locals, students, and alumni simply as "the W," Mississippi University for Women became the first public college for women in the United States when the state legislature chartered its predecessor, the Industrial Institute and College, on March 12, 1884, and located it on the campus formerly occupied by the Columbus Female Institute, a private college established in 1847. Today, Mississippi University for Women is something of a misnomer. Since 1982, men have attended the school as a result of a decision of the United States Supreme Court, which ordered the admission of a male student to the nursing program. Ironically, the most famous haunting at "the W" involves a beautiful young lady who came to the Columbus campus as a nurse in the early days of the Civil War.

Near the gated front entrance to the campus on College Avenue stands Callaway Hall, the university's oldest building. Known for its majestic clock tower, the stately edifice was constructed in 1860 as the clouds of war hovered over the South. During the great conflict that followed, Callaway acquired its resident ghost, known as Mary.

No one knows who Mary was or from whence she came. In the early days of the war, she simply showed up and volunteered as a nurse at Callaway, which by that time had been converted to a troop hospital.

In the course of her work ministering to wounded soldiers, Mary fell deeply in love with one of her patients. During the young man's convalescence, a romance blossomed, and the Southern cavalier asked Mary to become his wife. She gladly consented. But before the nuptials could take place, there was a war to fight.

Fully restored in body and invigorated in spirit by the thoughts of his forthcoming wedding, Mary's beau departed Columbus and rejoined his unit. Mary whiled away the long days of separation by engrossing herself in her duties. Her talents were sorely needed to care for the wounded and comfort the dying. A sense of hopelessness pervaded the place as the war dragged on. There seemed no end in sight for the pain, sorrow, misery, and destruction wrought by the hostilities. But Mary had her love to keep her going.

Unfortunately, the hand of fate was not kind. Mary's fiancé perished in battle. When the grim tidings were relayed to the nurse, she was devastated. Convinced that she had nothing for which to live, Mary slowly and deliberately made the long ascent of the six flights of steps leading to the clock tower surmounting Callaway Hall. In the tower, she affixed a noose around her neck and committed suicide.

Mary's ghost soon made her presence known in the building. And there she abides to this day.

In recent years, Callaway has been used as a dormitory for female students. A number of supernatural incidents and encounters at the residence hall have been attributed to Mary's ghost. For example, although the clock in the tower where Mary hanged herself is maintained on a regular basis, it often strikes thirteen times instead of twelve at midnight. Mysteriously, the clock breaks down every five years.

A painter working on the exterior of Callaway Hall and Columbus Hall—which is attached to Callaway in such a way that the two buildings appear to be one—was so frightened by Mary's ghost that he refused to complete his assigned duties. At the close of a day's work, the man chained and locked the door of Columbus Hall. He then climbed into his truck and, looking out the window, observed the spectral figure of a young woman in a long dress opening the very door he had just secured. She disappeared into the building. In a state of disbelief, the painter hurried back to the door, which was chained and locked, just as he had left it.

Residents of Callaway, particularly the girls on the fourth floor, commonly report eerie crying and moaning sounds late at night. They believe the phantom noises are made by Mary's spirit, which continues to mourn for her lost love.

Sometimes, Mary's ghost is a mischievous prankster. Students complain that their stereos are frequently turned on by a mysterious hand during the midnight hour. Some coeds have awakened in the morning to find that books and pictures have been pulled from their shelves and walls and piled in the middle of the floor by something other than human hands.

Mary's apparition has been seen in Callaway over the years. One such sighting was quite terrifying for one dorm resident. Late one night, the young lady was disturbed from her sleep by an overwhelming sense of unease. When the coed opened her eyes, she quickly glanced about her room and saw nothing out of the ordinary. Then she noticed an impression on her bed. It appeared as if someone had been sitting there. Fear overtook her, and the student cast her eyes from the bizarre spot. When she mustered the courage to look again, the indentation had vanished.

Exhaustion finally won out over fear, and the girl once again fell asleep. For a second time, she was awakened from her slumber. But this time, she felt something touching her face. Her eyes opened ever so slowly, only to see a misty white spectre floating above her face. Although her fright virtually robbed her of the ability to speak, the young lady managed a shriek that caused the ghost to vanish.

On a nighttime visit to the picturesque campus at Columbus, you might experience some of the other supernatural entities at "the W," such as the witches at work across the street from Martin Hall or the one-eyed ghost of Goen Hall. But if you happen to be taking a midnight stroll and hear the clock in the tower at old Callaway strike thirteen times, then you'll know that Mary, the university's most famous ghost, is alive and well—in the spirit world, at least.

Rebel Haunts

In 1861, just thirteen years after the University of Mississippi first opened its doors to eighty students, the state seceded from the Union and joined into a confederacy with its ten sister states of the South. Like many other colleges and universities throughout Dixie, Ole Miss—as the University of Mississippi is known to alumni and friends—was robbed of its student body due to the exigencies of war. Virtually every able-bodied student traded his schoolbooks for weapons of war and joined the small number of graduates already produced by the university to defend their homeland.

In the aftermath of the Civil War, Ole Miss students, proud of the valor displayed by the sons of the university on countless battlefields, chose to name their athletic teams the Rebels and selected "Colonel Rebel" as the school's mascot. Indeed, it seems that Ole Miss is inexorably tied to the conflict that engulfed the nation in the 1860s. And so are many of the ghosts that reside at the university. Most are thought to be the spirits of soldiers of "the Lost Cause," but the most notable ghost is that of the man said to be the greatest writer the South has ever produced.

Should you tour some of the oldest buildings on the picturesque campus in the quaint college town of Oxford, chances are you might hear or see ghosts of the Civil War.

At Ventress Hall, the late-nineteenth-century brick building named for the father of the university, a spectacular three-paneled stained-glass window sets the tone for a supernatural tour. Depicted in the window are the University Grays, a group of Ole Miss faculty and students who mustered for duty on the campus. Those men and boys ultimately fought as Company A of the Eleventh Mississippi Volunteers. By war's end, the company had suffered a casualty rate of 100 percent. While admiring the memorial window, you will probably get the distinct feeling that the Rebel soldiers in the magnificent work of art are staring at you. By the time you leave the nearby campus buildings that stood during the Civil War, you will most likely be certain that disembodied Confederates have been watching you!

At the head of "the Circle" on the historic campus stands the Lyceum. Completed in 1848, the massive Greek Revival edifice survives as the original building of public higher education in Mississippi. Every Confederate soldier who studied at Ole Miss attended classes in this building, which now houses the university's administrative offices. Staff members and students alike have heard unusual sounds coming from the far reaches of the structure. No one has been able to satisfactorily explain them. Some have attributed them to the spirits of the sons that the university provided for the Confederate war effort. As the theory goes, the soldierly spectres have returned to the place of their prewar happiness.

But there may be a more macabre reason for the hauntings in the Lyceum and nearby Farley Hall. During the Civil War, the Lyceum was used as a hospital for wounded and dying Confederate and Union soldiers from the Battle of Shiloh and other clashes in the area. Many of the soldiers treated in the building did not survive. Perhaps it is their ghosts who tarry here.

Even more ominous is the ground upon which Farley Hall rests. Erected in 1929 and now home to the Department of Journalism, the handsome Greek Revival structure occupies the site of a former Confederate morgue. A plaque reading "The Dead House" attests to the history of the site. At night, unexplained noises in the portion of the building that serves as a library have frightened numerous people. After working amid the supernatural sounds on the upper level of Farley for two weeks, one graduate student refused to ascend the stairs alone.

Also located on the main campus are several residential buildings inhabited by ghosts who are apparently not directly related to the Civil War.

At Deaton Hall, a dormitory housing a hundred men, the woman for whom the building was named is said to haunt it. Constructed in 1952, the residence hall honors Eula Deaton, the first woman to earn a master's degree at Ole Miss and the first woman to serve on the faculty of the English Department. Miss Deaton died before the building was erected, but her ghost has been encountered there on a number of occasions. When an elevator malfunctioned and trapped two students in 1985, Ole Miss officials attributed it to an electrical problem. However, dorm residents are sure that the ghost of old Miss Deaton did it.

Both a fraternity building and an abandoned sorority house are said to be haunted.

Saint Anthony Hall, the home of the Phi chapter of the Delta Psi fraternity, is inhabited by the ghost of a brother who died while returning from an Ole Miss football game at Louisiana State University. On occasion, his spectre has been observed standing in the fraternity's doorways.

The disembodied footsteps of a girl who died in the former Zeta Tau Alpha house can yet be heard on the upper floors of the structure late at night. When the sorority left the campus, its national headquarters sold the house to the university.

A leisurely thirty-minute walk east from the main campus will lead you to the site of the most famous haunting at Ole Miss. At the end of your walk, you will come face to face with Rowan Oak, the former residence of William Faulkner and now the home of his ghost and perhaps several others.

William Cuthbert Faulkner (1897-1962) has been acclaimed as the premier literary voice of twentieth-century America. Many scholars consider Faulkner the most studied author in all of literature. His life and works were deeply rooted in the South, and his abiding presence lingers at the primitive Greek Revival house where he lived and worked from 1930 until his death thirty-two years later. Ole Miss purchased the two-story white frame house from the author's daughter, Jill, in 1972.

Faulkner was a son of the University of Mississippi—although he did not graduate—and of Oxford, to which his family moved from nearby New Albany when William was four years old. The noted writer named his estate Rowan Oak for the Scottish tree by the same name in Sir James Frazier's *The Golden Bough*. In that book, the special tree wards off evil spirits and provides peace and privacy.

As he had hoped, Faulkner's Rowan Oak proved to be a place of peace and refuge where he could use his wonderful imagination to produce some of his greatest novels. But Faulkner was not able to chase away the ghosts at Rowan Oak.

Known to local children as "Mr. Bill," the author loved to entertain young and old alike by telling ghost stories on the front steps of his house. With children gathered around him on dark summer evenings, Faulkner would speak fast and in a low tone. His audience members would lean forward to hear every word, and at the perfect moment, the storyteller would scare the wits out of the children, all in good fun.

Faulkner's niece subsequently recollected many of the tales and published them as *The Ghosts of Rowan Oak: Faulkner's Ghost Stories for Children*. One of his supernatural yarns described a ghost that he and his family members had experienced at the house. Faulkner and his wife, Estelle, heard phantom footsteps throughout the house and eerie piano music coming from the parlor. Their children regularly reported the frightening sounds of a supernatural presence.

According to Faulkner, Colonel Robert Sheegog, the man who built the house in 1848, had a daughter who fell in love with a Yankee soldier during the Civil War. On the night when she attempted to elope with the dashing young officer, the unfortunate lady slipped and fell to her death. Thereafter, her ghost walked from her upstairs bedroom to her grave on the anniversary of her demise. On some occasions, the ghost played somber music in the house.

After the university acquired Rowan Oak, the house and the adjoining thirty-two-acre grounds were opened to the public so that the world might gain a better appreciation of Faulkner's life. Every year, more than fifteen thousand persons visit the estate, and some of them experience the ghosts. Colonel Sheegog's daughter has manifested herself in wraith-like form to visitors. Others have seen the ghost of an Indian whose land was taken to build the house.

A tour of the peaceful grounds weaves its way past cedars and hardwoods that were growing when the celebrated author lived and worked here. From time to time, Faulkner's ghost has been observed sitting in one of the trees or wandering about this private world he loved.

Lofty red cedars line a moss-covered brick walk leading to the house. On the interior, Faulkner's office has been left just as it was on the day he died. Handwriting—Faulkner's own script—decorates the walls. Here, he penned the outline of his Pulitzer-winning novel, *The Fable*. His old Underwood typewriter is on a small table near the window. The place looks as if the writer is still in residence. Indeed, his ghost is!

Staff members at Rowan Oak have heard male voices on the second floor when there was no one upstairs. On one occasion, loud banging and crashing sounds in Faulkner's bedroom sent staff scurrying there. Several items were found either broken or turned over, but no evidence of human intrusion was discovered.

Phantom footsteps, laughter, and a man's cries have been heard by estate personnel after the last visitor has left. There have even been reports that Faulkner's ghost has added writing to the walls. Perhaps this spectral script is from the novel that Faulkner intended to write before death came calling.

If a cold chill runs up your spine, if the hair on the back of your neck stands, if you start shaking at what you experience on a visit to the home of this true son of the South, your ghost host will be satisfied. After all, no one enjoyed scaring people with a ghost story more than did William Faulkner.

The Pride of Chowan

Little Chowan College, neatly tucked away in the northeastern coastal plain of North Carolina in the small, historic town of Murfreesboro, was unwittingly thrust into the national headlines in early March 2003 when the arrest of Khalid Shaikh Mohammed was announced. Mohammed, the suspected mastermind of the infamous September 11 terrorist attacks on America and a known lieutenant of Osama bin Laden, was a student at Chowan College for a brief period in 1984.

Despite the adverse publicity resulting from the arrest, the students, alumni, and friends of Chowan remain proud of their institution, which has been educating young people since 1848. It is the second-oldest of North Carolina's seven Baptist colleges. And one of its greatest sources of pride is its famous, loyal ghost, the Brown Lady of Chowan.

The McDowell Columns Building, the grand centerpiece of the Chowan campus, has long been the residence of the Brown Lady. The building was constructed in 1851, just three years after Chowan Baptist Female Institute—as the college was originally known—began operations here. It originally offered badly needed student housing in this rural, isolated part of North Carolina. It provided classroom and office space as well.

One of the students living in the Columns Building at the outbreak of the Civil War was the young lady now represented in the spirit world by the Brown Lady. Her name is lost to history, but she shall be called Julia for the purposes of this story. She was among the Chowan students who courageously stood up to a company of Confederate troops who sought to sequester the campus for military use in the second year of the war.

When the commanding officer demanded that Dr. Archibald McDowell, the head of the college, turn the buildings over to the Confederacy, Mrs. McDowell stepped onto the front porch of the Columns Building and queried why the soldiers had come to Chowan.

"Madame, we are sorry, but we must have this building for barracks," responded the officer.

In a tone evidencing her astonishment and displeasure, Mrs. McDowell replied, "What? You want us to close the doors of this school and send home our girls and teachers? No, it is impossible!"

Attempting to reason with her, the officer implored, "But madam, war is war, and we need the quarters for our men."

His pleas fell on deaf ears. In an instant, Mrs. McDowell turned to a teacher at her side and said, "Call the girls to me here!"

Hastily, Julia and her fellow students assembled in the face of the Confederate warriors. At their head was Mrs. McDowell, who said, "There are other buildings that can shelter you, but nowhere else can we carry on our work of educating these girls. I defy you, sirs—enter this building and you do so at the point of bayonet!"

Without further argument, the Confederates offered their salutes to the assembled women and marched away. This defiant stand and lesson in loyalty to the college made a lasting impression on Julia.

Almost miraculously, the school was able to keep its doors open to students for the duration of the war. But all was not well for Julia during that time. Her tall, handsome, Southern-born fiancé went away to fight— but to Julia's dismay, not for the South. As the war progressed, the young man was killed in battle. News of his death brought great sadness to Julia. Before war's end, she was dead also. Some say that she died of typhoid. Others insist that it was a broken heart.

Not long after Julia's death, the Brown Lady made her first appearance on the campus. A heavy snow had fallen in Murfreesboro on a cold Sunday morning. Because of the inclement weather, Dr. McDowell informed the students that they could worship in their rooms. He then made his way to his office, which was located directly across from his family quarters in the Columns Building. For a short time, he stood in the office doorway with a puzzled look on his face. Then, upon returning to the room where Mrs. McDowell was sitting, he asked, "Mary, who is that lady who came in the office a few minutes ago?"

With little apparent interest in her husband's question, she said, "No one."

Dr. McDowell continued, "Oh, but there was! A lady passed by me and whipped in and whipped out. As she came out of the room, she looked at me as though she was looking for someone. She had an anxious expression on her face, and she was dressed in brown."

Dr. James Delke, the professor of science and mathematics, made his way through the snow from his home to the campus later the same day. He immediately went to Dr. McDowell's office, were he found Mrs. McDowell. After greeting her, Dr. Delke queried, "Mrs. McDowell, who was that young lady just up here?"

As if parroting her response to Dr. McDowell, she remarked, "There was no one up here."

The bewildered professor then revealed his strange encounter: "When I came up the stairway, a lady dressed in brown came out of the parlor door and beckoned to me. She seemed to be expecting someone.

I went down the hall to speak to her and opened the parlor door. No one was there. I went to each door to see if she had gone out, but there were no tracks in the snow. I then went to the music room. No one was there. I opened the windows and looked on the porch but saw no tracks. Next, I went into the philosophical room and did the same thing, but I saw no tracks."

A change of seasons brought the return of the Brown Lady. One hot July afternoon while the students were away on summer vacation, Dr. McDowell was working alone in his office. He left his desk momentarily and proceeded toward the adjacent room. And there she was again—the same lady dressed in brown he had encountered before. She motioned for him to follow her, only to vanish before his very eyes.

Over the years that followed, numerous students and staff members witnessed the presence of the Brown Lady. They saw a mistlike female figure clad in a brown dress floating about the halls of the Columns Building. They answered phantom knocks at their room doors, only to find no human there. Upon unlocking the brick edifice for the start of a new day, custodians discovered hallways that had been perfectly clean when the building was secured the previous evening littered with leaves and debris.

The college has undergone many changes since the first appearance of the Brown Lady. In 1910, it acquired its present name. Male students were first admitted in 1931. Six years later, Chowan reverted to a junior college. It was restored to four-year status in 1992. But despite the myriad changes, the Brown Lady has continued to make her presence known.

During the 1940s and 1950s, the college actively celebrated its friendly spectre with the Brown Lady Festival. Each year, a student was selected to dress as the famous ghost, who had come to be regarded as a respected symbol of Chowan College.

In recent times, there have been reports of a number of encounters with the Brown Lady. She frequently attends theatrical performances, announcing her attendance by banging on metal pipes. And on at least one occasion in the 1990s, the Brown Lady was credited with preventing an assault on a coed. As the student was making her way to her dorm one dark night, she was accosted by an unknown assailant. Suddenly, the would-be attacker beat a hasty retreat for no obvious reason. After his apprehension, the suspect explained that he had fled the scene upon seeing a ghostlike form dressed in brown.

For nearly a century and a half, the Brown Lady has made Chowan College her home. The thousand men and women who comprise the student body do not fear her. Instead, they honor her as a source of pride and loyalty. So, if on a visit to the magnificent Columns Building, you should hear the distinct rustle of taffeta and see a misty figure summoning you, don't be alarmed. A nearby student will comfort and reassure you with these words: "Oh, that's the Brown Lady."

Emily

A simple tombstone, weathered by the often harsh winters of the North Carolina mountains, marks the plot in the Banner Elk cemetery where little Emily Draughn was buried many years ago. She died of tuberculosis at a tender age in Grace Memorial Hospital, which was then housed in the building adjacent to the cemetery on the campus of Lees-McRae College. Her faded grave marker bears a touching inscription: "She is not dead but sleeping." If numerous accounts of students and employees of Lees-McRae are to be believed, the spirit of Emily Draughn is very much alive on the campus of this small Presbyterian school nestled in the heart of North Carolina's ski country.

Tate Hall, a dormitory for female students, now occupies the four-story stone building that housed Grace Memorial Hospital from the early 1930s until 1964. Emily's ghost has been witnessed there, most often when many of the students were away on break. It's almost as if she comes back to look after the place where physicians and nurses cared for her during the last days of her short life.

Allison Norris, a former student who later served as the director of Tate Hall, experienced the supernatural antics of Emily's wraith, which she describes as a friendly, rather harmless trickster. In the course of her duties, Norris lived on the first floor of Tate with her husband. On one occasion, as a college break neared, she assisted one of the dorm residents, Misty Arpin, in the tedious chore of packing all of her clothes and belongings. Once the task was finished, the two left the room, and Misty locked the door. Later, she returned to discover that all of her things had been unpacked and placed in the closet and drawers. No roommate or other students had been present to perpetrate the prank.

Norris's husband, Craig, became concerned one evening while chatting with a security officer outside Tate when lights in the vacant building suddenly began to shift, as if room and closet doors were being opened and closed. When the two men rushed inside, they heard what seemed to be the entire Lees-McRae football team charging up and down the second-floor corridor. When the two men scurried up to that floor, the loud sounds seemed to rise to the third floor. A thorough search revealed no human presence in the building.

On two occasions, the floors of Tate seemingly changed positions before the very eyes of the Norrises.

In the late 1990s, the plumbing in Tate was replaced. In the course of the renovations, the Norrises painted their first-floor apartment. After the painting was completed, Craig and Allison walked up the steps to check on a room on the second floor. Then they proceeded up the steps to the third floor, but when they reached what should have been the hallway of the third floor, they found themselves on the second floor. Each floor is distinct and readily identifiable. The usually calm husband and wife stared at each other and hastily left the building.

Similarly, as the beginning of a new academic year approached, the Norrises posted the names of the students on their respective dorm rooms. After the process was completed, the couple happened to notice the specific name on the door of a second-floor room near the soft-drink machine at the end of the hall. When they made their way up the steps to the third floor, there were the same name and the same machine. It was if the second floor had ascended the steps with them.

Students living on the fourth floor of Tate have also detected Emily's presence. Emily Taylor, who served as a resident assistant in the dorm, was once disturbed by an unusual noise while she dressed in front of her mirror in her room on the top floor. She turned to ascertain the source of the sound. When she looked back into the mirror, the underwear she had just put on had been completely changed.

Other students on the fourth floor—which served as the hospital's maternity ward—have reported windows that opened and closed by themselves, as well as strange sounds like footsteps emanating from the attic.

Residents of Tennessee Hall and Virginia Hall, two dormitories, have also been visited by Emily's spirit on occasion.

An Australian member of the men's soccer team reported a mysterious blue light hovering in his room in Tennessee when electrical power was temporarily lost on the campus.

Over at Virginia, a female dorm, Katherine Anne Strickland suddenly awoke to see a white, cloudy shape floating across her room. On another occasion, she peered out her window to see the same cloudy form, this time much more distinct. It was the ghostlike figure of a girl strolling by the dorm in the direction of the campus bell tower. Yet a third time did Katherine Anne see the ghost. During a Christmas concert in Hayes Auditorium, she observed the spectre attired in a dress from a bygone era standing in the back of the hall. The apparition—that of a young girl—vanished into thin air.

Everyone familiar with the history of Lees-McRae knows that Emily's visits to the dorms are just that. Her permanent residence is the James A. Carson Library, located a short walk from Tate Hall. Staffers in the library are well acquainted with the mischievous spook. One security officer, having turned off all the lights in the building, was making his appointed rounds one evening. In the flash of an eye, every light in the place came on. He again extinguished all the lights, only to see them come back on in unison. After the eerie cycle was repeated another time, the aggravated man shouted in jest, "Emily, I'm tired. Please go to bed!" No more did the lights come on.

Library employees are accustomed to the regular reminders of Emily's presence. They sometimes hear a phantom voice. And on occasion, they watch with an understanding look as the elevator operates of its own accord.

At times, the ghost has even lent her assistance to staffers. Without question, the most remote part of the library is the area housing the Sterling Collection, the college's priceless Appalachian archives. Located in the far left corner of the second floor, the collection is open to permitted visitors only through a locked door beyond the library offices. When a rare volume was reported missing from the collection, the librarians conducted an extensive but fruitless search for weeks. At length, they concluded that the book had been misshelved. Sometime thereafter, while an assistant librarian was working in the stacks, her attention was drawn to a rustling sound that seemed to originate several shelves away. She called out, but when no answer came, the lady walked over to the place from whence the sound had come. No one was about, but there on the shelf, she saw it. The missing book was pulled out, its spine extending two inches beyond the edge of the shelf and the other books.

During the summer of 2000, Chuck Thompson, a student employee, had a rather chilling experience while shelving books in the same room where the missing volume mysteriously appeared. He looked up to see a woman examining some books at the end of the aisle. She had shoulder-length black hair and wore a black and white flowery print dress. Concerned that the person was in the secure area without permission, he hailed her, but she began to walk off. Calling out to the woman again, Thompson attempted to catch up with her, but she disappeared before his very eyes. As he hurried down to the first floor to tell his fellow workers about the strange encounter, his thumbs started bleeding at the base. Several colleagues witnessed the blood on his hands, which bore no nicks or cuts.

In 1931, Lees-McRae, originally built as a high school, became a full-fledged college dedicated to providing a higher education for the young people of the Appalachians. Not long after the college came into existence, little Emily Draughn died on its grounds. Though her premature death robbed the girl of a chance to study here, her spirit has availed itself of that opportunity for many, many years.

Of Ghosts Old and New

On January 15, 1795, the University of North Carolina began operations in Chapel Hill, thus making it the first state-supported university to open its doors in the United States. By the time the University of Georgia—the first public university to be chartered in America—opened, the venerable Chapel Hill institution had graduated seven classes. On the eve of the Civil War, Yale was the only American university to have a larger enrollment than Carolina, as the school is affectionately known to alumni and friends. Now in its fourth century of service to its state, the nation, and the world, the University of North Carolina has produced a long list of notable graduates, including James K. Polk, Thomas Wolfe, Charles Kurault, Andy Griffith, and Michael Jordan. Likewise, through its long and illustrious history, the university has acquired an interesting assortment of ghosts, both new and old.

In 1999, the American Society of Landscape Architects designated the 729-acre central campus in Chapel Hill as one of the most beautifully landscaped spots in the United States. One of the modern buildings to rise amid the magnificent trees and brick sidewalks at Carolina is the Paul Green Theatre. Named for the longtime professor at the school who won a Pulitzer Prize and invented the outdoor symphonic drama, the theater opened in 1978 and quickly became haunted by one of the old university's newest ghosts. No one is quite sure who or what it is. Eyewitnesses have described the thing as a fuzzy green light. It has most often been seen between the shop and the main performance hall. At other times, the eerie ectoplasm has been sighted at the stage-left portion of the auditorium. It appears to have the height of a normal human being.

Perhaps the unknown entity is the spirit of Paul Green, intent upon supervising the dramatic presentations in his namesake building. Or maybe it is the ghost of Charles Kurault. Following his death in New York City on July 4, 1997, the beloved American journalist was buried in the Old Chapel Hill Cemetery, located adjacent to the theater. Kurault's journalistic career began to flourish at the University of North Carolina when he was elected editor of the student newspaper, the *Daily Tar Heel*. No matter how far he roamed from his native state, the university in Chapel Hill was always home to him.

Near the western edge of the old campus stands the Carolina Inn. The hostelry was constructed in 1924 and given to the university in 1935 by John Sprunt Hill, one of its graduates. Sprunt called it "a cheerful inn for visitors, a town hall for the state, and a home for returning sons and daughters of our alma mater." Its charming exterior is that of a warm, inviting antebellum Southern plantation house with Neoclassical and Georgian features. Inside the massive brick structure, at least one room is haunted by a rather playful ghost.

Dr. William P. Jacocks, a physician with the International Health Division of the Rockefeller Foundation, retired to Chapel Hill in 1948 and took up residence at the Carolina Inn. There, the gentle, courteous man, known for his sense of humor and his fondness for practical jokes, lived in a room on the second floor until his death in 1965. By all accounts, his mirthful spirit continues to occupy his former quarters.

Over the years, numerous guests at the inn have been the objects of Dr. Jacocks's pranks. Most often, the complaints are that the entry lock on the room door will not work, even with the proper key.

In 1990, the room long occupied by the physician was extensively renovated and made a part of two other rooms. Not deterred by the changes, the ghost went about his antics. When a couple reported that the new electronic door locks would not work, the maintenance staff was summoned. After making unsuccessful attempts to open the door, the workmen were forced to climb a ladder in order to enter the room through a window. Ultimately, they had to remove the hinges before they could open the door.

A subsequent investigation of the haunted portion of the inn by a team of paranormal experts yielded recordings of the sound of footsteps in Jacocks's former quarters when the room was empty and secure. Also recorded in the vacant room were the sounds of a slamming door and of piano music. At the time, no piano was being played in the inn. Several words were likewise detected on the tape. Infrared video cameras captured the image of an orblike sphere floating through the room.

Carolina's most famous haunting traces its origins to the first third of the nineteenth century. By 1831, the University of North Carolina had established a reputation for academic excellence that extended beyond the borders of the Tar Heel State. That year, Peter Dromgoole traveled from his home in Brunswick County, Virginia, to Chapel Hill, where he enrolled at the university, which at the time admitted only male students. His first months of university life were marked by card playing, heavy drinking, and reckless behavior. But then Fanny came along, and his life was changed forever.

Fanny was the fairest of all the young ladies who lived in Chapel Hill. For Peter, she was love at first sight. Day after day, the infatuated couple met at the place favored by all young lovers in the university community. Piney

Prospect, as the place was then known, was a forested, isolated precipice that overlooked a deep valley just east of the campus. Their arms around each other, Peter and Fanny watched many pleasant, sunny afternoons fade into romantic evenings while seated upon a rock at the edge of the cliff.

To Peter's dismay, another Carolina student had an eye for Fanny. Although the young woman openly and repeatedly spurned the other man's advances, the rival for her affection persisted in his pursuit. His jealousy festered into an intense hatred of Peter Dromgoole.

Hoping to avoid a confrontation, Peter tried very hard to stay away from his avowed enemy. But one day on the then rather compact campus, the two students literally bumped into each other. As they passed, the rival slammed his shoulder into Peter with such force that the hat was knocked from his head. After bitter words were exchanged, the enraged aggressor challenged Peter to a duel. Determined to defend his honor, Fanny's beau accepted the proposal, for dueling was the method by which gentlemen settled disputes in those days.

On the warm spring night selected for the showdown, the combatants were accompanied by their seconds and other friends to the rock ledge at Piney Prospect. As the hour neared midnight, a bright moon beamed down upon the group assembled for the contest by pistols.

When the time was at hand, the onlookers took their distance as the two gunmen assumed their positions. Peter was a good marksman, but on that night he was not good enough. Almost as soon as the fire of the two guns broke the midnight stillness, the young Virginian began to stagger. Then he fell to the very ground where he and Fanny had shared so many blissful moments.

As blood poured from his fatal wound, Peter spoke lovingly of Fanny and his mother and lamented that he would die so young. His friends gently lifted his body and placed it upon the great boulder that had served as a bench for the lovers in happier times. Now, it was nothing more than a pall, for Peter was soon cold in death. His blood drenched the rock.

Fearful of the consequences that might follow from their participation in the deadly affair, the seconds and other members of the dueling parties decided to keep the matter secret among themselves. Evidence of the duel had to be buried. Thus, the group dug a grave, interred Peter's corpse in it, and covered the burial site with the bloody rock.

On the morrow, Fanny showed up at the appointed time at the place where the lovers regularly rendezvoused. Peter was nowhere to be seen. She returned each day, but her boyfriend was not there to embrace her. Inquiries to university officials about the missing student produced no clues as to his whereabouts.

Fanny fell into severe depression. Her emotional instability weakened her body to the point that she could no longer make her daily visits to Piney Prospect. She spent her final days at her home, where she sat in a chair gazing out a window in a trancelike state. Death soon followed.

Not long thereafter, the spectres of a young couple began to be observed at Piney Prospect on moonlit nights. The sightings continue to this day.

Piney Prospect, now known as Glandon Forest, is little changed from the time of Peter and Fanny. It is a perfect setting for a ghost story or a mystery tale. The great boulder on which Peter's lifeblood drained is still there. It rests in the shadow of spooky Gimghoul Castle, an actual stone castle built here by a secret society in the 1920s.

From the rock, the view is magnificent. Far below runs a stream known appropriately as Fanny's Creek. When it rains, the ancient stains on the great boulder are said to run blood-red. After studying the legendary rock, university geologists concluded that the red discoloration was nothing more than copper deposits.

Not even the best scientists from this prestigious institution of higher learning can explain the presence of the ghosts that roam the enchanted forest. Yet anyone familiar with the bittersweet tale of Peter and Fanny will readily understand that the apparitions in Glandon Forest are supernatural reminders of the intangible human qualities of love and honor.

From Old East, the oldest public university building in America, to some of the most modern and sophisticated research laboratories in the world, the campus of the University of North Carolina is a wonderful blend of old and new. So, too, are its ghosts.

UNIVERSITY OF SOUTH CAROLINA
COLUMBIA, SOUTH CAROLINA

Terror Below

During the war with Iraq in 2003, Americans were fascinated by television accounts of the intricate complex of tunnels that run under the surface of Baghdad. Not surprisingly, then, few places on Southern campuses are more mysterious to the public than the off-limits tunnel systems that snake their way under the buildings and streets of many colleges and universities. Most of the tunnels were built as heat shafts or utility service areas. Yet despite their rather mundane purposes, the subterranean passages have become the source of numerous ghost stories, folk tales, urban legends, and the like.

Because access to the dark, often eerie man-made caverns is strictly forbidden, they have taken on a sinister, haunted atmosphere. While most of the reports of supernatural occurrences and entities in the tunnels have little basis in fact, the accounts of the strange humanoid creature said to inhabit "the Catacombs" under the University of South Carolina have a hint of credibility.

Established on December 19, 1801, the University of South Carolina has been the centerpiece of Columbia, the state capital, for two centuries. Running under much of the 351-acre campus is a maze of heat and utility tunnels collectively known as "the Catacombs." No one knows who or what the terrifying inhabitant of the Catacombs is or how, why, or when it came to take up residence in underground Columbia. But a number of believable eyewitness accounts of the unusual being provide a physical description of it.

According to university records, the first reported encounter with the underground dweller occurred on November 12, 1949, when two students spotted what they described as "a strange man dressed in bright silver" in the road near the Longstreet Theatre, a campus landmark built in 1855 at the corner of Greene and Sumter Streets. Before the astonished fellows could hail the thing, it lifted a manhole cover, descended into the depths below, and replaced the cover.

As it turned out, Chris Nichols, one of the witnesses, was a reporter for the *Gamecock*, the student newspaper at the university. Nichols promptly informed his readers of the sighting of what he dubbed "the Sewer Man." However, no other eyewitness accounts were forthcoming over the next few weeks, so the frenzy created by Nichols's article subsided, at least temporarily.

On April 7, 1950, a campus security officer was on routine patrol when he discovered the remains of two mutilated chickens scattered behind the Longstreet Theatre. His initial reaction was that fraternity boys had littered the theater's loading dock with the feathers and pieces of chicken during a prank, hazing, or rush activity. In accordance with procedure, the officer radioed a report from his nearby squad car. He then returned to the back of the theater building, where he found a silver man bent over the chicken scraps. Shining his flashlight on the bizarre being, the policeman was shocked at what the beam revealed. The thing was staring at him. It had a repugnant face, hideous in both shape and color. And then the officer saw it. At the center of the weird creature's forehead was a small third eye!

Badly shaken by this one-on-one encounter in the darkness, the officer hastened to his radio and called for immediate assistance. After promptly responding to the plea for support, the policeman's colleagues accompanied him to the rear of Longstreet. There, they saw nothing unusual, other than some chicken feathers and bones strewn about the loading area. Overcome with emotion, the officer whose two eyes had met three carefully described the creature to the others, vainly attempting to persuade them to believe him.

Almost twenty years passed before another credible account of the creature came to light. On an October night in the late 1960s, some fraternity members chose to use the Catacombs as the site for a pledge ritual. From Gambrell Hall, the home of the History Department, several brothers and three pledges descended into the tunnels and proceeded west toward the Horseshoe, the historic original portion of the campus. Law-enforcement records indicate that no sooner had the students turned the first corner than they happened upon what was described as "a crippled looking man dressed all in silver."

Curiosity gave way to terror when "the Silver Man" suddenly attacked the young men with a metal pipe. According to the police report describing the incident, Matthew Tabor, one of the pledges, was thrown to the floor and sustained "minor cuts and minor shock." Taking immediate flight, the students exited the tunnel and promptly notified university police of their strange encounter. A subsequent search of the Catacombs by a cadre of law-enforcement officers yielded no evidence of the underground dweller.

In order to prevent future incidents in the tunnels, the university went about closing off the entrances. Students, faculty, and the general public were warned that the Catacombs were not to be accessed. Nonetheless, several sightings of the Sewer Man/Silver Man/Third-Eye Man were reported in the 1980s and 1990s. Although university officials tended to discredit the reports, maintenance workers on the campus are very wary of the tunnels and use them only when absolutely necessary.

Students who attempt to venture into the tunnels under the University of South Carolina face expulsion, and other unauthorized intruders face prosecution for trespass. Access has been prohibited in order to prevent accidents in the underground world below the campus. The university policy has nothing to do with the ogre who once roamed the tunnels. After all, the Catacombs have been sealed off for many years, so the creature, if it ever existed, died of starvation long ago. Or did it?

Should you leave the theater on a dark night after a wonderful evening of drama, the man dressed in silver and sporting a third eye who you encounter at the intersection of Greene and Sumter might just be someone or something other than an actor from the Longstreet stage.

WINTHROP UNIVERSITY
ROCK HILL, SOUTH CAROLINA

Pitchfork Ben

On bright, sunny days, Tillman Hall, the imposing administration building of Winthrop University, casts an expansive shadow over the entrance to the hundred-acre campus in Rock Hill, South Carolina. And on some days, a spectral figure has been observed staring from the front portico of the towering Romanesque structure. No one at Winthrop questions the identity of the apparition that roams the oldest structure at the school. Benjamin Ryan Tillman (1847-1918) was the guiding force behind the creation of Winthrop University, and it seems his spirit continues to reside in the building that bears his name.

Ben Tillman's two terms as governor of South Carolina stretched from 1890 to 1894. He championed the cause of industrial, agricultural, and technical education in the Palmetto State. His efforts produced

Clemson Agricultural and Mechanical College (now Clemson University) and Winthrop Normal and Industrial College (now Winthrop University), the former for boys and the latter for girls. When the cornerstone of Tillman Hall—originally known as Main Building—was laid in 1894, Tillman was on hand to offer the keynote address.

Winthrop was in its infancy when its students learned that Ben Tillman was true to his nickname of "Pitchfork Ben." How Tillman came to acquire a moniker often associated with the devil remains a subject of debate. One legend holds that he picked it up after his left eye was gouged out by a pitchfork thrown by an angry slave. Evidence, however, indicates that Tillman lost his eye to disease just after he volunteered as a teenager for service in the Confederate army in July 1864. A farmer by vocation, Tillman may have earned the nickname as a result of his devotion to agricultural pursuits and his interest in the agrarian lifestyle. But in all likelihood, "Pitchfork Ben" came into being when Tillman went to Washington, D.C., in 1895 to begin the first of his four terms as a United States senator. Though they were both Democrats, Senator Tillman and President Grover Cleveland were avowed opponents. As he prepared to embark on his work in the nation's capital, the fiery and colorful South Carolinian said this about Cleveland: "He is an old bag of beef, and I am going to Washington with a pitchfork and prod him in the ribs." In 1902, the Senate censured Tillman, then the only farmer in that body, for assaulting another senator on the floor.

Even though Ben Tillman was embroiled in national politics at the very time Winthrop was educating its first students, it seemed to the young women in the student body that the reach of his pitchfork extended to the campus of "his" new college in northern South Carolina. In accord with Tillman's wishes, the Winthrop catalog specified that the school would close for only four holidays: Thanksgiving Day, Christmas, Washington's birthday, and the May birthday of Robert C. Winthrop, the man for whom the institution was named. Explaining Tillman's rationale for the policy, the catalog noted, "This arrangement is made to save parents extra railroad fare, and to prevent the serious demoralization and loss of time to the students and the disorganization of

College work always consequent upon the breaking up of the school within three months after the opening of the sessions." Thus, when a lady arrived at the Rock Hill campus, she came prepared to stay until May.

Winthrop was but ten years old when the students organized a campaign that put them at odds with Pitchfork Ben Tillman, the man they considered the embodiment of Ebenezer Scrooge. With the assistance of their parents, the young women presented to the Winthrop Board of Trustees their case for ending the hated restriction against an extended Christmas vacation. Alas, their pleas fell on deaf ears, for Pitchfork Ben was a veteran and influential member of the board.

Unwilling to abandon their crusade, the protestors took the matter to the state legislature.

In Washington, Ben Tillman was outraged with the Winthrop students when he learned that the South Carolina House of Representatives had voted to abrogate the harsh vacation policy. He fired off a series of letters to his friends in the South Carolina Senate imploring them to dismiss the proposed changes as sheer nonsense.

At Columbia, the leading newspaper in the state capital took a jab at Pitchfork Ben when it decried to its readers, "Winthrop is not Senator Tillman's private college; it belongs to the people of the state . . . and the sentiment about the full family circle at Christmas time should have consideration."

Soon thereafter, the state senate, by a slim majority of three votes, passed a bill that required at least ten days of vacation during Christmas for all South Carolina college students. By appealing to the state legislature, the Winthrop students of the late nineteenth century had pulled one over on Pitchfork Ben.

Over the years, those young ladies and generation after generation of subsequent students, both female and male, have passed in and out of Tillman Hall and the other hallowed buildings on the campus. But Pitchfork Ben endures in the very building where he gave birth to the university.

Tillman Hall did not gain its current name until 1962, when the

Tillman Science Building—also named in honor of Ben Tillman—was razed. Today, it continues to dominate the Winthrop landscape. Even without regard to the reported sightings of Pitchfork Ben's ghost on the covered porch of the massive brick structure, its dark, somber exterior hints at its haunted nature. A tall clock tower surmounts its four stories, and lesser spires adorn the adjoining wings.

If the glaring spectre of Ben Tillman does not greet you as you enter the front door of the venerable edifice, the portrait of Pitchfork Ben is there to welcome you as soon as you set foot in the dimly lit foyer. The rare painting is affixed to the left wall near the door. Only a white handkerchief, the white collar of his shirt, and the flesh tones of Tillman's grim, sinister face brighten the otherwise dark portrait. Here is perhaps the only artistic rendering of the college's founder that exhibits more than a profile of the one-eyed man. But even in this painting, a distinct shadow cloaks the left side of Pitchfork Ben's face.

Some people claim that the portrait has supernatural elements about it. Tillman's right eye seems to follow all those who dare to enter his building. And then there were the recurrent nightmares experienced by a Winthrop employee not long after she accepted a position at the university in the 1970s. She confided in her coworkers the details of her terrible dreams, which involved ghosts and an eerie portrait that she had never seen. After the lady carefully described the portrait seen in her sleep, her colleagues escorted her to the painting of Pitchfork Ben. Much to her dismay, it was the same portrait as in her nightmares.

Bizarre, unexplained sounds are heard throughout the building by employees and visitors alike. Most seem to originate from the fourth floor, the clock tower, or the basement. Skeptics dismiss all supernatural explanations for the noises, attributing them to the natural expansion and contraction of the wood used to frame the old building. But some employees and others familiar with Tillman Hall are not so sure. As Bill Culp, the longtime director of the university's physical plant, pointed out, "Ben Tillman was so intent on this building. We think the ghost may just be hanging around to make sure that the place is being kept in good condition." A former editor of Winthrop's minority newspaper noted,

"Tillman's haunted. You can feel the presence of something there. If you step toward the fourth floor, you can feel something."

Since the 1940s, the fourth floor has been closed for lack of safety exits. It contains a winding maze of empty rooms, save for some discarded pieces of furniture and a few bird skeletons. The old wooden floors creak and groan at the touch of a human step. A door leads to the tower steps.

When they must work in the building at night, some employees choose to mask the strange sounds coming from above and below by playing their radios at full blast. Granted, the emptiness and darkness of the fourth floor add to their unease, but it may be that what lies beneath them is even more disconcerting.

In the basement of Tillman can be found old wooden stocks that were used to punish prisoners who misbehaved while the building was being erected. Convict labor was instrumental in the construction process. Legend has it that Pitchfork Ben himself whipped, bludgeoned, and forked some of the disobedient prisoners who were placed in the stocks. Members of the building's cleaning crew now hang their coats on the remnants of the dark past. One college official remarked about the basement, "The ghost probably lives in the building's dungeon, where the prisoners were kept, or in the tower."

To all those unfamiliar with the history of Winthrop University, Tillman Hall at first glance appears to be nothing more than an old building much like those found on many a college campus in the South. But a closer look might reveal a phantom staring from the entrance or a passing shadow on the top floor or in the tower. Not to worry, though. It's only Pitchfork Ben Tillman keeping his eye on his university.

The Life, the Loves, and the Ghost of a Southern Belle

If Margaret Mitchell's famous fictional character Scarlett O'Hara ever walked the South in flesh and blood, then surely it was in the form of Adelicia Acklen of Tennessee. And now the ghost of the intriguing, wealthy, and controversial Southern belle roams the fabulous antebellum mansion that Adelicia built in Nashville in the 1850s. Indeed, Scarlett's famed plantation house, Tara, pales in comparison to Adelicia's opulent Belmont Mansion, which serves as the haunted centerpiece of the campus of Belmont University.

No one knows exactly when the ghost of Adelicia Acklen took up residence in the lavish Italianate palace that survives as the second-largest pre-Civil War mansion in the South. And likewise, it is not exactly certain why Adelicia's ghost haunts the massive thirty-six-room structure, which contains two floors of some 10,900 square feet and a basement of 9,400 square feet.

Speculation is that her supernatural presence lingers here because of a common human frailty: greed. Some historians have acclaimed Adelicia the wealthiest lady of her time in the South. As the theory goes, she could not part with her vast riches when death came calling.

Others, however, believe that there is a more tragic reason for the haunting of Belmont Mansion. Despite her great affluence, Adelicia suffered many tragedies, including the deaths of nine of her ten children and two of her three husbands. Maybe the wraith waits here in vain for the lost loves of her life.

A third explanation for her ghost has to do with the mansion itself. During its construction, Adelicia spared no expense. Her grand salon has been deemed the most elaborate domestic room ever built in Tennessee, and the mansion holds the largest collection of nineteenth-century cast-iron ornaments in the United States. In recent years, Belmont University has undertaken extensive restoration efforts at the palatial estate. Maybe the ghost tarries here to ensure that no harm is done to the home that Adelicia named *Belle Monte* because it was sited on one of the highest hills in Nashville.

Perhaps the mansion's ghost is as complex as the lady it represents. Born to a prominent Nashville family on the ides of March in 1817, Adelicia Hayes was a lady of privilege and social prominence all of her life. She married three times, each time for a different reason. According to historians, her first marriage was for love, her second for business, and her third for the hell of it.

At the age of twenty-two, Adelicia took her first husband. Isaac Franklin, an extremely wealthy businessman and planter, was twenty-eight years her senior. Despite the disparity in their ages, the Franklins enjoyed a romantic marriage that produced four children. Sadly, none of the children lived beyond eleven years, and Isaac died after seven years of marriage.

Although Adelicia inherited an enormous fortune from her first husband, she wanted more. She challenged Isaac's will and prevailed. As a consequence, the young widow was a millionairess by the time she was thirty years old. Her holdings included stocks, bonds, a cotton plantation of eighty-seven hundred acres in Louisiana, a farm of two thousand acres in Tennessee, a vast tract of thirty-eight thousand acres in Texas, and 750 slaves.

Adelicia weighed only ninety-five pounds, but her diminutive size belied her tough demeanor in the business world. Ever anxious to grow her wealth, she acquired large parcels of land in Nashville through shrewd speculative ventures.

In 1849, Adelicia married Joseph Acklen of Huntsville, Alabama. Highly regarded as an astute businessman, Acklen was required to execute a prenuptial agreement before Adelicia would marry him. Soon after their marriage, they began planning Belmont Mansion, which took several years to build.

When the sumptuous villa was completed in 1853, it was elegantly decorated with the finest of furniture and artwork. A 105-foot brick tower was built to irrigate the spacious grounds; it still stands today. Estate dependancies included a 200-foot-long greenhouse, a bear house, and a zoo of imported animals such as monkeys and alligators.

Six children were born to the Acklens, including twin daughters named Corinne and Laura, after Adelicia's two sisters. Within days of each other, the two little girls died of typhoid at the age of two. Devastated by the terrible loss, Adelicia spent countless hours in the room where they had slept. She claimed that their laughter could yet be heard there.

More tragedy was soon to follow. At the outbreak of the Civil War, Joseph Acklen left Nashville for New Orleans, where he intended to protect the family's extensive cotton holdings. Almost a year passed before Adelicia heard anything about her husband. When the news came, it was terrible. Joseph had died of pneumonia.

Although she was grief-stricken by the revelation, Adelicia realized that her business affairs must be kept in order. She promptly set out for Louisiana, traveling at great risk through the conflict-ridden South. Using her incomparable charm and guile, Adelicia duped troops from both armies in order to salvage twenty-eight hundred bales of cotton. At one point in her grand charade, she convinced Confederate forces to escort a Yankee wagon train filled with her cotton to New Orleans, which was under Union control. There, in defiance of prevailing military law, the Acklen cotton was loaded on a ship bound for England. From the deal, Adelicia pocketed a cool million. In the words of one of her sisters, Adelicia "could talk a bird out of a tree."

Two years after the war's end, Dr. William Cheatham, a renowned Nashville physician, became Adelicia's third husband. Two thousand guests attended the lavish wedding at Belmont. But wedded bliss was not to be. Some years after she married Dr. Cheatham, Adelicia had serious regrets. In time, she asked him to leave the mansion. He took up residence in a local boardinghouse.

After Adelicia died of pneumonia in 1887, her grand estate was sold. Gone forever were the galas at which she had reigned as the queen of the South. But no one would take her place as the grande dame of the house.

In the wake of Adelicia's death, Belmont Mansion became the home of Belmont College, a school for women that operated here until 1913, when its successor, Ward-Belmont, took over. In 1951, Ward-Belmont gave way to Belmont University, a private liberal-arts institution affiliated with the Baptist Church. Thirty-three hundred students attend the university today.

Guided tours of the mansion on the campus are available for a fee. Should you have an opportunity to visit the estate, do not be surprised if you feel the presence of, or even witness, the spectral lady of the house, just as have many students and officials of Belmont over the years.

Paintings of some of Adelicia's children who died at an early age are found throughout the mansion. At or near these portraits, many people have been overwhelmed by the strange sensation that they were being watched.

Visitors have reported the sound of phantom footsteps behind them while descending the stairs after a visit to Adelicia's bedroom. A glance to the rear has revealed no human presence, and the footsteps have stopped when the visitors stopped walking. Once the descent resumed, so did the disembodied footsteps.

Because the mansion was the site of extravagant holiday celebrations, there is little wonder that Adelicia makes her presence known during the Christmas season, when the university holds special events there. Footsteps like those of a woman pacing to and fro have emanated from Adelicia's vacant chamber as students prepared for the festivities.

University employees and construction workers have been frightened and aggravated by Adelicia. On one occasion, a Belmont staffer was allowed to live in a room near the main hall of the great house. Unexplainable nocturnal noises about the place were so terrifying that the lady abandoned her quarters.

While attempting to renovate Adelicia's bedroom, laborers were frustrated by several supernatural interferences with their work. One man's tools were lost when a wall abruptly fell without apparent cause.

Skeptics may scoff at the idea that these strange sounds and occurrences are evidence of the ghost of Adelicia. After all, old houses—even mansions—creak and groan and settle as they age.

But how do the skeptics explain what eyewitnesses have seen in Belmont Mansion? During an examination period in the 1960s, several friends were absorbed in their work in a room in the mansion that had been set aside as a study lounge. Having gained permission to work beyond curfew, the girls labored late into the night. Suddenly, their attention was drawn to an apparition that appeared before them. Attired in an elegant white gown, the female spectre with black hair radiated beauty. Awed but not frightened by what they saw, the girls attempted to follow the wraith, but it disappeared into thin air.

Without question, the most intriguing encounter with Adelicia took place when a student attempted to get photographic evidence of one of the most famous legends on the Belmont campus. As the legend goes, a certain mantel clock in the mansion stopped ticking at the very moment Joseph Acklen died. Thereafter, when the clock was placed on the mantel of his sitting room, it would operate perfectly. Only when it was removed again would it malfunction.

When the university yearbook photographer snapped a picture of the ticking clock just after it had been placed on the mantel, he captured on the film more than he had bargained for. On the developed prints, there appeared the image of a lady attired in a hooded cloak. There had been no such person in the room when the snapshot was taken, and there was no evidence that the film had been tampered with in any way.

A symbol of the Old South, Belmont Mansion survives on the campus of this small university in the Tennessee capital. It was built to be the home of one of the most colorful, manipulative, glamorous, and affluent belles that Dixie has ever known. And by all accounts, the spirit of Adelicia Acklen is still alive and well at her beloved *Belle Monte*.

Spooks Galore

For almost a century now, East Tennessee State University has been providing a quality education to young people, many of them from the mountains of Tennessee and North Carolina. Throughout the school's history, most of its sixty thousand graduates have studied and lived with ghosts. There are few buildings on the Johnson City campus that are without a spook of some sort. Indeed, East Tennessee State University is regarded by a number of paranormal experts as the most haunted institution of higher learning in the South.

Gilbreath Hall, constructed as one of the original buildings when East Tennessee State opened in 1911, is the logical place to begin a ghost tour of the campus. Named for Sidney Gordon Gilbreath (1870-1961), who served as the first president of the school, the stately brick edifice is now used as a classroom, office, and theater building. President Gilbreath, a strict moralist and disciplinarian, selected the exact spot where "his" building now stands. His ghost continues to monitor the daily activities there and to take care of the place.

Employees assigned to Gilbreath Hall affectionately refer to the helpful revenant as "Uncle Sid." When a storm threatens the campus, open windows in the building abruptly close on their own. If staff members leave doors unlocked by mistake or forget to turn lights off at the close of a workday, Uncle Sid is often credited with remedying the oversight.

Sometimes, in his desire to save the school money, the ghost prematurely shuts off the utilities. For example, a cast member of a theatrical production in Gilbreath Hall was hastily removing makeup between acts when the lights and water in his dressing room were shut off without apparent reason. Frustrated by the freak incident, the student screamed for Uncle Sid to turn the lights back on. No sooner had the words been spoken than the dressing room was ablaze with light.

At least one student has seen Gilbreath's ghost. From the window of her room in nearby Carter Hall, a coed from Bristol, Tennessee, cast her gaze toward Gilbreath Hall at two o'clock one morning. She was frightened to see standing at an attic window a ghostlike figure of a man bathed in red light.

Uncle Sid has also been heard in the building's attic. After detecting strange noises coming from above the ceiling of the upper floor one evening, a dean of the graduate school asked a member of the custodial staff to assist him the following day in searching for the source of the mysterious commotion. When the two men crawled into the low attic, they discovered a pair of framed pictures. One was a rather large photograph of Abraham Lincoln and the other an engraving of a chief of the Cherokees. They had been stored in the attic since being removed from the downstairs office that once belonged to President Gilbreath. As the dean examined the dusty items, he felt something brush lightly against his shoulder, and he heard a faint whisper saying, "Thanks, from Uncle

Sid." At the time, the custodian was not close by.

Named for Charles C. Sherrod (1882-1967), the second president of the school, the 192,000-square-foot Sherrod Library is haunted by the ghost of a former librarian.

By their very nature, the library stacks at most universities are creepy. But the catacombs of books at East Tennessee State are especially scary. They hold the matronly wraith of a lady who had little tolerance for horseplay or noise in her facility. Library employees working alone in the stacks often report the uneasy feeling that they are being watched.

One student staffer actually saw the Sherrod spook while going about her duties in the stacks during Christmas vacation. After locating the volume for which she was searching, the coed turned to go up the steps and was startled by what was descending—or floating—down the staircase. It was the corpse of a bespectacled old woman, attired in a maroon dress of a bygone era. She had no legs! Frozen by fear, the student could only watch as the stern-faced woman glided along the steps and vanished.

No one knows who or what haunts Mathes Music Hall. But the custodians assigned to the building readily attest that ghosts are present throughout the expansive brick structure. Unnatural cold spots are found at various places inside Mathes. And when the building is closed for the day, the spooks go to work with the cleaning staff. Workers frequently report the sounds of phantom voices and disembodied footsteps. One evening, a loud crash reverberated all over the building. No sooner had a thorough search revealed nothing out of the ordinary than a second crash caused the entire building to shake. No damage was subsequently discovered, nor was a cause.

Burleson Hall is thought to be haunted by the spirit of Christine Burleson, a nationally renowned Shakespeare scholar who taught English at East Tennessee State for many years. In the 1970s, in the twilight of her career, the popular professor was stricken with a debilitating disease that ran in her family. Confined to a wheelchair and unwilling to become a burden to others, she took her life. Since her death, her ghost has been experienced in the building where she taught countless students.

Her voice and her dreadful moans sometimes echo down the corridors. Her floating apparition has even been sighted here.

And then there is the haunted portrait of Christine's father, David Sinclair Burleson. Campus tradition holds that when you look at the portrait, the eyes of Burleson seem to follow you. But the eyes are not those of Mr. Burleson. Rather, they are the eyes of Christine!

Yoakley Hall, once a dormitory, now serves as a campus office building. Its ghost is said to be that of a coed who committed suicide by leaping from a window on the top level of the four-story brick structure. Following her tragic death, numerous people have reported feelings of unhappiness and depression while occupying or working in the room from which the unfortunate girl jumped. On more than one occasion, a spectral figure has been observed leaning out of the very same room.

Students who reside on campus not only attend classes with ghosts but live with them as well. Dorsett Hall is haunted by Nell Dorsett, the lady for whom it was named. Dorm residents consider old Nell something of a prankster. She often locks students out of their rooms, and she turns water on and off in the bathrooms. Sometimes, when phones in the building are answered, no human is at the other end. Unusual cold spots abound throughout the old building.

Located on the west end of campus, Lucille Clement Hall houses female students—and an assortment of spooks. While taking a shower very early one Saturday morning in an otherwise unoccupied bathroom, a coed was distressed to hear heavy breathing. She looked out of the stall, but no one was about. Quickly, she finished her bathing and stepped out, only to discover that her clothes were not hanging where she had put them. At length, they were found in a nearby corridor.

Other residents of the same dorm have been frightened by an elevator and fire doors that open and close by an invisible force. Some believe the ghost to be that of Lucille Clement and refer to the spook as "Lucy." More than one coed has awakened in her room to discover someone or something standing over her.

Residents of Lucille Clement have long complained of the mysterious sound of marbles falling on the floor above them. Many have been frightened by this phenomenon in the middle of the night. Several explanations have been posited for the supernatural noises. One tradition tells of a young boy who was trapped at the building site when the basement foundation was laid. By throwing his marbles, he vainly attempted to notify would-be rescuers before his body was encased in cement. In a similar vein, another story holds that a child dropped one of his marbles while playing on a beam in the building. He fell to his death while attempting to retrieve it. A divergent explanation is associated with the past use of the building. Lucille Clement Hall once served as a hospital facility. As the tale goes, a nurse accidentally dropped a patient with marbles in his hands. The child died as a result of the fall. For whatever reason, the sound of falling marbles continues to haunt the young ladies who reside in the dorm.

Windows in Lucille Clement yield a spectacular view of the ROTC tower that stands in a nearby field. In the last quarter of the twentieth century, a depressed student hanged himself from the tower. Since that time, the shadowy form of a hanging body has been observed by young women peering from their dorm windows.

Ghosts also inhabited campus buildings that no longer stand. Cooper Hall, for example, was demolished in 1984. University officials publicly stated that the cost of projected renovations was exorbitant, yet some folks familiar with the history of the building are sure that Cooper was taken down because college employees were too scared to work there. But that's another story, for there are plenty of spooks to go around in the buildings that stand on the campus of this most haunted university.

TENNESSEE WESLEYAN COLLEGE
ATHENS, TENNESSEE

A Spirited Romance

Some Southern colleges are haunted by events that transpired on their campus sites long before the schools came into existence. Such is the case with Tennessee Wesleyan College, a small Methodist institution of approximately eight hundred students. Although the school has been an integral part of Athens—a town of fifteen thousand in the eastern part of the state—since 1857, the ghosts here came to be in the latter part of the eighteenth century.

A state historical marker on the Tennessee Wesleyan campus is the only tangible reminder of the bittersweet human drama that unfolded on these grounds during the tempestuous days of the Revolutionary War.

140

In 1756, this portion of Tennessee was the exclusive domain of the Cherokee Indians, despite the incursion of British military forces who attempted to build and maintain outposts at strategic geographic sites. One such installation was Fort Loudon. A tenuous peace between the British intruders and the Indians came to an end in February 1760, when the Cherokees laid siege to the fort. For six months, the people trapped inside the outpost subsisted on meager rations, but they were ultimately forced to surrender when starvation became a certainty.

Assured that their offer of surrender had been accepted, the emaciated men, women, and children set out on the trek from Fort Loudon to Fort Prince George. En route, the Indians launched a brutal, unprovoked attack on the defenseless group. Most of the unsuspecting, unarmed people were annihilated. One woman, however, was spared as a result of her impassioned plea to Chief Attakullakulla. She and her tiny son were taken to the village of the Overland Cherokees, where they were adopted into the tribe.

In time, the chief married the white woman, and she bore him a beautiful daughter. They named her Nocatula Cooweena. As the years passed, "Weena," as the girl came to be called, grew into a woman of ravishing beauty, great charm, and wonderful personality. Her irresistible beauty caught the eye of every brave in the tribe.

One of their number meant to have Weena as his wife, no matter what the cost. Mocking Crow was a rather cocky, callous young man for whom Weena had little regard. Despite the gifts that he lavished upon her family and the magnificent athletic prowess he exhibited before her father, the pretty Indian princess wanted nothing to do with him. She openly rejected his marriage proposals on more than one occasion.

True love came into Weena's life when one day during the Revolutionary War her father and some of his men returned with a badly wounded British soldier they had come across during a hunting trip. Weena was immediately taken by the handsome young man. She joined with other women in the village to restore him to health. Meanwhile, the infatuated nurse and her patient fell madly in love. Some members of the tribe suspected that Attakullakulla would disapprove of his daughter's relationship with the soldier. To the contrary, the chief was overjoyed because he had come to admire the stranger's courage and strength of character.

When the soldier proposed to his princess, she accepted with delight, and her father gave his blessing to the marriage. After the two became one, Weena's father bestowed a special name upon his new son-in-law. Because the British fellow stood tall and proud, he was called Connestoga, which meant "oak."

Although happiness surrounded the newlyweds, all was not well. Overcome with anger wrought by rejection, Mocking Crow vowed revenge. Nothing short of the demise of Connestoga would satisfy him. His opportunity came only days after the marriage ceremony.

Connestoga and a number of his adopted Cherokee brethren set out on a hunting expedition. In advance of the party, Mocking Crow secreted himself in the undergrowth in the area where Connestoga and the others planned to hunt. Upon their arrival, the British man gave chase to a deer that disappeared into a thicket. When some nearby bushes began to rustle, he believed he had located his prey. Instead, Mocking Crow lurched toward Connestoga with a razor-sharp knife. Before the unsuspecting victim could resist, the brave slashed his throat.

Rushing to the aid of their fallen comrade, the hunters saw that life was quickly ebbing from Connestoga's body. Anxious to get word back to the village, the fleetest of the braves set out on a furious race. He reached Weena, delivered the doleful tidings, and then accompanied her to the scene of the vicious attack.

Connestoga was yet clinging to life. Weena, tears flowing down her cheeks, knelt beside her husband and grasped his cold hand. She used her other to tenderly rub his face as she begged him not to leave her. But death would not be denied. As Connestoga closed his eyes, Weena screamed that she could not live without him. Then she caught sight of the weapon used to slay her husband. Taking hold of the bloody knife, Weena thrust it into her heart and joined her soul mate in death.

When Weena's heartbroken father arrived at the site, he offered prayers and the Indian rituals for the burial of the dead. Braves were then instructed to bury the bodies at the spot of the tragedy, rather than transport them to the village for interment. Offering a final farewell to his loved ones, Attakullakulla placed an acorn in the hand of Connestoga. In that of his dear daughter, he nestled a hackberry seed.

Before many years passed, two seedlings sprouted from the very ground where Connestoga and Weena were buried. And before the aged chief died, he took great pride in the oak tree and the hackberry tree that stood side by side at the grave site.

When the burial ground became the campus of Athens Female College—the predecessor of Tennessee Wesleyan—in the mid-nineteenth century, the two trees were not harmed. Instead, as the story of the real-life lovers who went to the grave together was told by generation after generation of students, the trees became an amorous spot where many campus romances took root and blossomed. But then in 1945, the hackberry was stricken with disease, thus forcing college officials to take it down. After Weena's tree was removed, the oak mysteriously began to wither and die. It was cut down five years later.

Even though nothing more than a metal sign now marks the historic spot on the campus, romantics will tell you that the spirits of Connestoga and Weena yet abide here. For many years, there have been sightings of two spectral figures floating about the place where the trees once grew. Ghostly voices and phantom whispers have often been heard here. Those who have experienced the supernatural presences report that they are not hostile or frightening. Instead, they are comforting.

There are few campus sites in the South that are more romantic than this special one at Tennessee Wesleyan College. For here, when hand-holding lovers hear what others believe to be only the rustle of a gentle breeze or see what others believe to be mere shadows, they know what it really is. It is simply a reminder from the spirit world that true love cannot and will not die.

A Very Haunted Hill

Although the University of Tennessee did not acquire its official name until 1879, its roots can be traced to Blount College, which was chartered in 1794, two years before Tennessee became a state. Blount College was succeeded in 1807 by East Tennessee College (not to be confused with East Tennessee State University in Johnson City) at the original college site on the corner of Gay Street and Clinch Avenue in downtown Knoxville. Two decades later, the campus was relocated to a permanent site on a promontory just west of town. College trustees, citing their reasons for the selection of the new location, noted, "The shape of the hill, the commanding view from it and to it in every direction . . . render it a site as eligible almost as the imagination can conceive."

Long known as "the Hill," the historic central portion of the University of Tennessee campus is haunted by a wide array of supernatural entities. During the Civil War, virtually every campus building on the picturesque site overlooking the Tennessee River was destroyed. From the ruins emerged the modern University of Tennessee. Most of the existing structures clustered about the Hill boast a ghost.

Among the lesser-known haunts are those that inhabit the McClung Museum. The museum was built atop a sealed Indian cave, and Indian spirits are said to roam the facility.

Similarly, at the General Counseling Center, located on Lake Avenue in a house once owned by John A. Thackston, the university's former dean of education, staff members frequently encounter the ghost of Dr. Thackston. Doors open and close at will, and the spectre of the old dean sometimes strolls the house.

And then there are the phantom, bloodcurdling screams often heard in Hess Hall. These frightening sounds are attributed to the restless spirit of a student who committed suicide in the residence hall in the mid-1970s.

Each Halloween season, Reese Hall hosts one of the most popular haunted-house attractions in the entire state to raise funds for charitable causes. Most of the visitors who enjoy being terrified by the make-believe creatures lurking throughout the building do not realize that Reese Hall is home to very real ghosts every day of the year. Shadowy figures have been seen peering from the windows of the building, and face-to-face encounters with apparitions have been reported in the corridors, rooms, and basement of the dormitory. An early-nineteenth-century cemetery that was located near the structure is believed to be the source of the hauntings.

And then there are the university's most famous ghosts, found at a quartet of sites on and about the Hill.

Completed in 1931, the James D. Hoskins Library served as the main campus library for almost forty years. In 1969, it became the repository for the special collections of the university. Dwelling in the vast recesses of the building is the ghost of William Jesse, a former library director, who reportedly took his own life. On numerous occasions, library staffers and patrons have observed his apparition in the archives section, the very place where Jesse spent most of his time.

If the mouth-watering smells of beef stew and cornbread suddenly waft through the Hoskins Library, you can be sure that the ghost of Evening Primrose is about. No one really knows whether she was a student, an employee, or a faculty member. Her spectre has been seen wandering the stacks, knocking off books as she goes. At times, the revenant plays havoc with the library elevators.

Over at the Tyson Alumni House, acquired by the university in 1954, the haunting is said to be that of an animal. Long regarded as one of the finest homes of old Knoxville, the early-twentieth-century three-story mansion was the home of Lawrence Tyson, a World War I general, attorney, industrialist, and United States senator. When the university purchased the estate, it agreed to maintain the only grave located on the grounds, that of the Tyson family dog, Bonita. Apparently, Bonita's playful spirit refused to leave the mansion after her owners departed.

General Tyson bought the little dog for his daughter while traveling in Puerto Rico. When the beloved animal died, she was buried in a grave plot now enclosed by chains at the rear of the house. Employees in the old mansion have from time to time detected a supernatural presence moving about the place. They have heard phantom footsteps and unexplained noises. Most blame the mysterious occurrences on Bonita, whose ghostly form still scampers about the place she called home.

Strong Hall was built to honor the life and memory of Sophronia "Sophia" Strong, who died in 1867. A half-century later, her son, Benjamin, donated the site of his mother's home—one of the first brick dwellings constructed in Knoxville—to the university with several conditions attached: Strong Hall would be built on the land; it would house only female students; and a wildflower garden would always be located on the grounds. The first part of Strong Hall was completed in 1923. Since that time, the university has honored its promise to the Strong family. And for as long as anyone can remember, the dormitory has been the site of the university's most famous haunting.

During her life of fifty years, Sophia Strong, the wife of a respected Knoxville physician, gave birth to twelve children. It seems that Sophia, known far and wide for her motherly instincts, left a matronly spirit at the site where she nurtured and reared her large family. Generations of Strong Hall residents have benefited from the care and concern of their supernatural housemother. When tempers flare between students in the dormitory, Sophia, as the ghost is known, always seems to appear to defuse the heated situation.

On one occasion, a disagreement between two coeds resulted in a rather ugly shouting match. At the height of the verbal salvos, one of the girls stopped speaking completely, as if to concede the war of words. But when her adversary saw the terror in her opponent's eyes, she knew something was terribly wrong. Turning around, she saw it, too. There was the apparition of Sophia, wearing a stare of stern disapproval.

Unless she is needed to resolve a confrontation between residents, Sophia can usually be seen only on her birthday, February 17. Tradition has it that if you look into a dorm mirror on that day, you will see her spectre wearing a long white dress.

Even when Sophia cannot be seen at Strong, her presence is felt. Sometimes, she plays tricks on the girls by locking them out of their bathrooms. But despite her occasional antics, no one disputes the ghost's desire to look after the girls of Strong. When those eerie balls of light suddenly appear and float down the corridors of Strong Hall, the residents know that old Sophia is making her nightly rounds.

The last of the haunted places about the Hill is not a building but rather the site of an old burial ground.

Because of the destruction wrought by the Civil War, the oldest structure on the Hill, South College Hall, dates to 1872. But some of the most famous spooks here predate that structure. On November 29, 1863, the Battle of Fort Loudon was fought on the Hill. Among the many Union soldiers killed in the battle was General William P. Sanders. Fort Loudon was subsequently renamed Fort Sanders. Many of the Yankee soldiers who perished in the battle were laid to rest at a burial site on the Hill. Subsequent construction disturbed their graves and their spirits.

Spectral figures clad in blue uniforms are frequently observed wandering around the old battle site. Sometimes the *tramp, tramp, tramp* of marching troops echoes across the campus. Sounds of phantom gun battles have also been reported.

On your visit to the campus of the University of Tennessee, should you happen to hear an animal-like cry that makes your hair stand on end, rest assured that it's only the phantom wolf said to prowl the grounds. After all, you'll have enough to worry about on this very haunted hill.

Ghosts-in-Residence

When Texas Tech University opened its doors to 914 students on September 30, 1925, there was cause for great celebration in Lubbock and environs. Finally, western Texas had a science college. Texas Tech ranks as a Johnny-come-lately among the storied universities of the United States. Nevertheless, during its first three-quarters of a century of operation, the school has written a supernatural history second to none.

Holden Hall, located on the main part of the 2,008-acre campus, attracts many visitors, who come to see the thirteen-hundred-square-foot mural adorning its walls. In 1954, nationally known artist Peter Hurd completed the masterpiece, which depicts the history of western Texas from 1890 to 1925. While admiring the spectacular artwork, some people have noticed a kindly, old gentleman standing nearby. His dress—including a Stetson hat—harks back to a different time. Indeed, he is a ghost from Texas Tech's past.

Campus historians believe that this apparition is the spectre of the founder of the Chemistry Department at the university. Highly respected as a scholar, the professor was a bespectacled man of slight build who sported a well-groomed beard. His keen desire to be a friend to the young people enrolled at the university enabled him to forge a bond of trust with his students. He freely gave many hours of his time to tutor pupils who needed extra help in their quest to master the complex lessons of chemistry.

A pall of sorrow enveloped the Texas Tech community when a mysterious illness claimed the life of the professor. Everyone grieved because the university had lost one of its best friends and teachers.

Or so they thought.

Since his death, the good professor has returned periodically in spirit form. Not only has his apparition frequently been seen in Holden Hall, but it has also made numerous appearances in the study halls of Tech's fraternities and sororities. For decades, students have reported improved grades after nighttime visits by the ghost of the old prof, who continues his tradition of service even after death.

One of the most influential persons in the early growth and development of Texas Tech as one of the premier universities of the South was its first president, Paul Whitfield Horn. And today, his ghost abides on the campus to which he devoted the last years of his life.

The Ex-Students Association, a part of the Merket Alumni Center, is located in the building that served as Horn's home during his tenure as university president. It was here that Horn died of a heart attack after finishing his morning bath on Wednesday, April 13, 1932. Although it is unclear whether he died in his upstairs bedroom or the adjacent hallway, there is no question that his spirit has never left the house.

Employees of the Ex-Students Association jokingly refer to the resident ghost as "George," but they know who it is. They have smelled phantom smoke from the cigars, pipes, and cigarettes that President Horn enjoyed smoking in the house, which is now a smoke-free building. They have heard the eerie sounds of jingling keys as his ghost made his way down the hallway. Humanlike chatter has been heard in rooms that are vacant.

Even in the light of day, some staff members have been unnerved by the supernatural presence in the building. One business manager experienced the feeling that someone was walking behind her and running his fingers along her neck when no one else was about. A chapter-development assistant has not only smelled spectral tobacco smoke in her office, which was Horn's bedroom, but has also witnessed the tray in a new copy machine jump from time to time. Attempts by repairmen to stop the sudden violent movements of the tray have been unsuccessful.

When darkness overtakes the Texas Tech campus, the former president's house is closed for business. But people inside after hours have reported strange goings-on. A number of custodial workers, claiming that the place was haunted, quit their jobs after working only a few nights in the old building. A reporter for the Texas Tech student newspaper who courageously spent the night of Friday the thirteenth in the house alone reported that he heard the venetian blinds being raised in Horn's bedroom.

On the third floor of the Geoscience Building, the hauntings are of a more ominous nature. In 1967, Sarah Morgan, a cleaning lady, was killed by a scalpel-wielding student in a biology laboratory. Apparently, the crazed young man made his way into the building to pilfer a copy of a final exam, only to be surprised by the custodian.

Until the murderer was captured and brought to justice, the Lubbock campus was in a state of uproar. Finally, things quieted down, and Sarah's ghost made her first appearance. Several semesters after the tragedy, the shadowy likeness of the slain worker was observed peering through a classroom door as students were taking midterm exams. Since that time, her spectre has made regular appearances on the third floor during examination periods. Her ghost is said to project sympathy for the students as they pore over their work.

There is another supernatural reminder of the ghastly murder. In the laboratory where Sarah Morgan was killed, a stain that has been washed away many times mysteriously reappears on each anniversary of the custodian's death. Her blood is said to have stained that spot on the floor.

Wandering the maze of utility tunnels under the Texas Tech campus is said to be the ghost of a male student whose amorous ways cost him his life. In order to make secretive visits to Horn and Knapp Halls, both girls' dorms, the young buck used the subterranean passageways to the buildings. After an ever-vigilant housemother discovered the intrusions by the playboy, the university maintenance staff was summoned to weld the tunnel entrances shut.

When the tomcat set out on his next nightly prowl, he was dismayed to find that the underground access to the dorms was no more. As he made his way back through the labyrinth, his flashlight went out. In the absolute darkness, he became disoriented. For days, the terrified boy roamed the blackness in his desperate but unsuccessful quest to find his way to safety.

During one sorority initiation ritual, some pledges were required to place food at the tunnel gates in the basements of Horn and Knapp. Upon inspection of the sites the following day, the girls found that the food had vanished. Maybe custodians removed it, or perhaps it was taken by someone or something. After all, various coeds have reported seeing the apparition of a handsome but rather gaunt young man standing at the gates.

Should you need directions to a particular building on this campus on the plains of western Texas, you might ask a professor, the university president, a custodian, or a student for assistance. If no answer is forthcoming, it is most likely because you have encountered one of the ghosts-in-residence at Texas Tech University.

Of Brenda and Wanda

Fun, camaraderie, youthful high jinx, and parties are often associated with life in college dormitories. There is also a serious side to life in residence halls: the countless hours of study, the anxiety over examinations and grades, and the numerous personal problems associated with college life. And sometimes, life in dorms ends in tragedy. At the University of North Texas, two residence halls are haunted by the ghosts of a pair of young ladies whose lives were cut short under dreadful circumstances.

Founded in 1890, the university now has more than 27,000 students, ranking it among the five largest institutions in the state university system. Maple Street Hall, a coed dormitory housing 668 students, is the second-oldest building on the North Texas campus. Its ghost, named

Brenda, came into being as a result of a mysterious murder that shocked the campus and the entire city of Denton.

In the early-morning hours of September 25, 1981, Brenda Brandenburg, a freshman, left a party at Kerr Hall. Moments later, she was savagely attacked by an unknown assailant between the Methodist Youth Ministry Center and her dormitory. Her lifeless body was later recovered in a golf-course parking lot near the Radisson Hotel. Death was attributed to strangulation. There was no evidence of sexual assault. Although law-enforcement authorities believed that the murderer was most likely an employee of the university, no one was ever arrested for the crime.

Shortly after Brenda died, supernatural things began to take place at Maple Street Hall. They continue unabated to this day.

As far as anyone knows, Brenda's ghost has never done physical harm to any of the dorm residents, but her presence has terrified many students. Brenda's former room at Maple Street is a hot spot for the wraith's activities. Late one night just before the opening of the fall semester in 1995, Jill Spencer, a resident assistant at the dorm, carefully turned the lights off and closed the door to each room as she inventoried the hall assigned to her. In the process, she heard a telephone ringing in a room that she had already checked. Because none of the rooms was yet occupied, Spencer assumed that the ringing was a wrong number and would end momentarily. But on and on it went. Finally, to put an end to the vexing, incessant noise, she made her way to the room from which the sound came. To her dismay, the door was open and the light was on. At the very moment she walked into the room, the ringing stopped.

Mystified by the bizarre occurrence, Spencer hurried downstairs to relate the experience to a colleague, at which time she was informed that Brenda's ghost resided on her hall.

A year later, Jill Spencer was once again witness to Brenda's ghostly activities. Because of the supernatural forces at work in the deceased girl's room, no one was assigned to live in it when the fall semester rolled around in 1996. Nonetheless, two students who lived in an adjacent room came to Spencer to inquire as to the identity of their suite mate. The roommates told their resident assistant that they had knocked on the door of the room on several occasions without response. When Spencer informed the coeds that the room was vacant, she could see the visible signs of fear that suddenly overwhelmed them.

They reasoned with Spencer that somebody must be sharing their suite, since they had heard water running in the shower of the suite bathroom every morning and had found the shower wet upon subsequent inspection.

So as not to increase the girls' terror, Spencer refrained from relating the story of Brenda. Rather, she grabbed the master key and escorted the coeds to the "vacant" room. Although not exactly sure what they would find when the key turned the lock, Spencer opened the door. All were greatly relieved to find an empty room. Then they looked at the floor. Leading from the shower to the closet were wet footprints! Cautiously, the three women proceeded to the closet and opened it ever so slowly. There was nothing inside, save a puddle of water on the floor.

Residents of Brenda's floor have become all too familiar with the mischievous, sometimes playful activities of the revenant. Some coeds find it impossible to keep their wall art hanging right side up. Other young ladies have difficulty sleeping when Brenda is about. Televisions, radios, and stereos mysteriously come on and blare in the middle of the night.

Ghostly pranks aside, no one at Maple Street Hall who has seen Brenda's spectral face has ever forgotten the sheer terror that it instills. On occasion, dorm residents have actually observed Brenda's face peering out of the glass-paneled emergency door located near the very spot where the unfortunate student was attacked.

Bruce Hall, a dormitory for 486 students who have a special interest in the fine arts, is a lively place because of the frequent jam sessions and lectures there. But Bruce also has its dark side. Its ghost, known as Wanda, is a grim reminder of a sad occurrence that took place in the building's attic in the first half of the twentieth century.

Wanda was a resident of Bruce Hall who discovered during the fall semester that she was pregnant. Fearing the reaction of her parents, the unmarried girl decided to forego a trip home during Christmas vacation. Instead, she hid in the attic of Bruce Hall to sort out her problems.

During her days of loneliness, she brooded in a chair by the attic window overlooking the deserted campus. Finally, she made a decision. Wanda attempted to abort the child by herself, but she died of internal bleeding in the process. Her body was removed from the building after school resumed several weeks later. Yet her spirit lingered. For more than fifty years, Wanda has been the most famous ghost at North Texas. Her abiding supernatural presence has been felt, heard, and seen at Bruce Hall.

As might be expected, the attic, located above the fourth floor of Bruce, is off-limits. Wanda's ghost is said to dwell there. Residents of the dorm's top floor often hear strange sounds—footsteps, heavy dragging noises, crying, and human voices—filtering down from the "unoccupied" attic.

As if the eerie discordance from above is not enough, Wanda frequently comes visiting on the fourth floor. Coeds have complained that full cans of hair-care products have been emptied mysteriously in the night. More than one girl has felt an invisible hand tugging at her earring. Some have even reported seeing a girl dressed in dated clothing roaming the corridor.

During school breaks, Wanda's activities on the fourth floor seem to intensify. Resident assistants who watch over the dorm while the students are away have detected a wide variety of paranormal activities. In one instance, a female resident assistant was found by her colleagues cowering in a shower, fully clothed, crying and badly shaken after a round of checking rooms on the fourth floor.

A male staff member then began the process of checking each room. When he opened the first door, the blinds in the room abruptly fell to the floor. Considering this nothing more than a freakish incident, he moved on to the next room. After the same thing happened a third time, he began running down the hallway. As he passed door after door, the blinds came falling down in each room. In the course of his mad dash to safety, the young man experienced the sensation that something or someone was brushing against his ear.

While checking the rooms on the fourth floor on another occasion, the same male resident assistant noticed a girl standing in the corridor. Calling to her, he asked what she was doing in the building. No answer was forthcoming. Rather, the stranger turned and made her way around the corner. Cognizant that the hallway terminated in a dead end, the fellow gave chase. But to his dismay, the girl had simply vanished.

During a thirty-minute foray into the dark attic, a paranormal investigator found a single piece of furniture—a chair by the window. On bright, moonlit nights, some folks claim that the silhouette of a young woman sitting in that chair can be seen in the attic window of Bruce Hall.

Why do Brenda and Wanda continue to haunt their residence halls at the University of North Texas? No one knows for sure, but perhaps they are in search of the fun and frivolity of college life that they were denied.

Texas Gothic

Of the many architectural landmarks on the University of Texas campus in the state capital, two structures are unique because of age or height. Located on the west side of the campus is the Littlefield Home, a spectacular Victorian mansion thought to be the university's oldest structure. At the very heart of the campus stands the imposing 307-foot University of Texas Tower, the tallest building at the school. In addition to their architectural distinction, these two buildings are known for their ghosts.

George Washington Littlefield (1842-1920), the man who gave more money to the University of Texas during its first half-century of existence than any other individual, built the magnificent house that bears his name. A native of Mississippi, Littlefield grew up in Texas and proudly served as an officer of the famed Texas Rangers during the Civil War. Following the great conflict, he amassed a king's ransom as a cattle baron, banker, and land speculator. In 1893, he constructed for his wife, Alice, a grand Victorian palace on an Austin avenue that was lined with such structures. Now, it stands as the lone survivor of that bygone era on the edge of the original forty-acre campus. Its appearance presents a stark contrast to the other campus buildings, which exhibit primarily Spanish Renaissance and modern architectural styles.

From the porch of the sumptuous mansion, George and Alice Littlefield could watch students walk to and from classes during the early years of the university. But that was when George was at home. His vast business enterprises often required him to be away from Austin for extended periods. During those absences, Alice spent much of her time in the attic, whether by force or by choice. Now, her ghost roams there and in other parts of the house, which was donated to the university when Alice died in 1935.

One tradition holds that George locked Alice in the attic while he was away in order to "protect" her from the men who strolled by the house. While imprisoned there, she was repeatedly attacked by the bats that claimed the space as their own.

A divergent story insists that Alice, of her own volition, whiled away her lonely hours in the attic. There, she watched and waited for the return of her George. Over time, Alice's fear for the safety of herself and her husband deteriorated into depression, paranoia, and insanity. The horrible screams of terror that are sometimes heard coming from the attic are attributed to the ghost of Alice.

By simply viewing the exterior of the house, one might suspect that it is haunted. Its towers and turrets give the place a shadowy, creepy aura. The small, round window in one of the attic turrets is of particular interest. On occasion, the spectre of Alice has been observed peering out, as if watching for George's return. At other times, the window is shuttered. Curiously, that window can be accessed only by crawling through the attic and into a rather narrow hole that leads to the interior of the turret.

Now used by the university for special events, the house is a spooky place for employees. Its dark Victorian interior, highlighted by ornately carved hardwood and pine, offers the perfect setting for a ghost story. Even when they know that no one else is in the house, staffers have the uneasy feeling that they are not alone. None of the employees enjoys being the first to enter the house in the morning or the last to leave it at day's end.

Alice's ghost moves furnishings in the mansion from time to time. For example, when event planners returned to work after a holiday, they found that two candelabra had been removed from the fireplace mantel and placed in the middle of the parlor floor. During the holiday period, the building had been locked tight.

Alice gave birth to two children, but both died as infants. Ironically, it is children who often perceive the presence of her ghost. When the four-year-old granddaughter of a staffer walked into the house for the first time, she promptly remarked, "Someone is dead here." Another employee, after working late at the mansion, snuggled her eight-year-old granddaughter, only to have the child say, "Granny smells like a ghost."

In 1937, the University of Texas Tower was constructed to stand as the centerpiece of the campus and to serve as an enduring symbol of academic excellence and personal opportunity. When its carillon played its first tune, "The Eyes of Texas," no one could have foreseen that the tower would become the site of one of the greatest crime dramas in American history. Ghosts linked to that memorable tragedy are said to linger in and around the tower.

In the predawn hours of August 1, 1966, Charles Joseph Whitman, Jr., a former Marine and Eagle Scout, killed his mother and his wife at their respective residences in Austin. Then, about eleven-thirty that morning, the twenty-five-year-old man—an architectural engineering student at the university—made his way up the tower. With him, he carried a footlocker filled with six guns, seven hundred rounds of ammunition, knives, food, and water. Stopping at the twenty-eighth floor, he proceeded to kill the receptionist in anticipation of barricading himself on the observation deck at a height of 231 feet. When Whitman heard people ascending the stairs from the twenty-seventh floor, he opened fire, killing two and wounding the others.

By noon, all was ready for Whitman to carry out the deadly attack about which he had fantasized. Alone on the observation deck, he indiscriminately began shooting innocent victims who were walking about the university campus. For almost ninety minutes, his reign of terror continued unabated. Finally, at 1:24 P.M., a courageous band of two police officers and a deputized private citizen successfully made its way onto the circular deck, where Whitman was confronted and shot to death, thus ending the nightmare. By that time, sixteen people lay dead or dying and another thirty-two were wounded.

A note penned by Whitman before he ascended the tower that day requested that an autopsy be performed to ascertain if he had been mentally ill. Pathologists subsequently found a small tumor on his brain, but medical experts disagreed as to whether it had caused him to go on the killing spree.

Following the terrible incident at the tower, strange things began happening there. By all accounts, they continue today. When security officers turn off the interior lights and lock up, the lights sometimes mysteriously come back on as the guards walk away. After he had to turn the light off several times one night, a highly vexed officer exclaimed, "Charlie, let's get along!" The lights promptly went out and stayed out.

After a young man jumped to his death from the observation deck in 1974, it was closed to the public for many years. Once extensive renovations were made and security precautions were put in place, it reopened in 1999. Now, visitors are once again afforded a breathtaking vista of the campus and the surrounding capital city. Here, too, is the same view of passersby that Charles Whitman had on that fateful day in 1966.

At night, the exterior of the tower is bathed in orange and white lights, the school's official colors. Special light patterns are programmed for athletic events, the Fourth of July, and commencement.

During one commencement, the tower light display mysteriously began to turn on and off. No other explanation being available, some people claimed that it was the work of Whitman's ghost.

Spectral figures have been observed roaming the grounds surrounding the tower at night. Phantom screams have been heard in the same area when the structure was ablaze with its special lighting. Could these supernatural sights and sounds belong to the restless spirits of the unfortunate men and women who lost their lives on the landscape here?

A haunted Victorian mansion and a tower of death—what more can a university offer for a true Gothic experience?

Waiting for a Second Chance

Perhaps it's only a coincidence that Wayland Baptist University, a pioneer in the study of parapsychology, has a ghost in its administration building. Or maybe it's simply poetic justice.

In either case, this small liberal-arts school of a thousand students was one of the first two American universities—the other being Duke University—to begin parapsychology research in the twentieth century. And Wayland researchers had to look no farther for a case study than Gates Hall, the majestic centerpiece of the eighty-acre campus in Plainview.

Supernatural forces have been at work on the third floor of this Colonial-style brick building for many years. As far back as 1940, the ghost of Phoebe, as she will be known for the purposes of this story, has been at work in Gates Hall. Since its completion in 1910, the stately structure has been a versatile building, having earlier served as a dormitory and as the home of the Music Department.

Phoebe was a Wayland music major who could sing as well as play the piano and the flute. For months leading up to her final examinations, or music jury, the young lady could be heard rehearsing hour after hour, day after day, on the third floor of Gates.

When the day of decision was at hand, Phoebe gave her utmost to showcase her musical talents to the jury. Alas, her performance was not good enough, and she failed. Overcome by a sense of defeat and hopelessness, the forlorn girl made her way to the third-floor balcony of Gates, from which she jumped to her death.

To this day, Phoebe's spirit is said to meander the halls and rooms of this venerable building in an endless effort to hone her skills as a musician. University officials admit there are sounds in the sturdy edifice that cannot readily be explained. When Gates is devoid of human occupants, students and faculty alike have heard a phantom singing voice. Others have detected the sounds of a rehearsal by a single musician in the empty structure. All attempts to locate the source of the eerie music have been unsuccessful. Investigators have found doors locked to the rooms from whence the mysterious notes have come. The same doors were known to have been unlocked prior to the search.

During much of the last quarter of the twentieth century, the third floor of Gates was abandoned to Phoebe's ghost. It was used for little more than storage. When workers began renovation efforts on the floor in the late 1990s, they uncovered an unusual stain on the floor. Since it resembled the shape of a coffin, the men assumed that a casket of some kind had been stored there for a long period in the past. Rumors began that Phoebe's ghost had slept there until the construction activity disturbed her. There was no denying that once the third-floor project began, the laborers frequently found themselves inexplicably locked out of the work area.

Phoebe's spectre has been seen by a number of people. At times, her lonely figure has been observed through the windows of Gates. Inside the building, the shadowy apparition of a young lady attired in a flowing white dress has been encountered wandering the hallways.

A security guard assigned to Gates had a terrifying experience with the resident ghost as he made his rounds one evening. His curiosity was aroused when he noticed the lights burning on the third floor. Ordinarily, that portion of the building was dark. Hurrying to investigate, he turned a corner, and there she was—a ghost wearing a white gown. For a brief moment, the man stood motionless in abject fear. According to the official report he subsequently filed, the spectral form looked unearthly, giving off a strange luminosity. As soon as he regained his composure, the guard fled the scene.

By all accounts, Phoebe's ghost is not a malevolent spirit. So never mind if you happen to hear ghostly music or come face to face with a glowing lady in white on a visit to Gates Hall at Wayland Baptist University. It's only the ghost of Phoebe, who's rehearsing for the day when she will have another chance with the jury.

Haunts of a Historic Kind

Located in the old colonial capital of Williamsburg, the College of William and Mary boasts an impressive list of superlatives and historic milestones: the school is the only institution of higher learning in the United States to have a Royal charter; it is the second-oldest college in the United States, after Harvard; and it was the birthplace of Phi Beta Kappa, America's most prestigious academic honor society. Indeed, William and Mary is steeped in history and tradition. And a part of that great tradition is its ghostly lore.

More than seventy-five years before the Declaration of Independence was signed, the Sir Christopher Wren Building was erected on the new campus of the College of William and Mary. Tradition has it that the structure, completed around 1699, was designed by Wren himself, the noted English architect behind St. Paul's Cathedral in London. Regarded as the soul of the college, the majestic brick edifice was virtually destroyed by a trio of fires in 1705, 1859, and 1862. Nonetheless, it survives today as the oldest academic building in continuous use in the United States. And not surprisingly, it is also the oldest haunted building on a college campus in the nation.

As the Revolutionary War was nearing a successful conclusion for Virginia and its sister colonies at nearby Yorktown on the Tidewater peninsula, the Wren Building served as a hospital for wounded American and French troops. Once the three-and-a-half-story edifice was returned to academic use, William and Mary professors and students began to hear disembodied footsteps on the upper floors. To this day, the same bizarre sounds are heard.

Some believe that the phantom footsteps belong to a French soldier who died in the Wren Building as a result of wounds sustained in the fight for American independence. But there might be another explanation for the haunting. Sir Christopher Wren's spirit may be at work.

In the middle of his discourse at a night class in the building in 1967, a professor was interrupted by overhead noises that sounded to be heavy footsteps. Concerned that there might be an intruder in the building, which was supposed to be otherwise empty, the professor paused long enough to conduct a precursory search of the upper floors with his class. After they found no one, he resumed the lecture. Once again, the footsteps were heard. Deviating from his prepared lesson, the instructor quipped to his students that Sir Christopher Wren must be inspecting his building. No sooner had the words left his mouth than a thunderous crash sounded from above. Fearing that a chandelier had fallen in an upstairs hallway, the professor and his students once again searched the premises. They found nothing out of the ordinary.

Over at Phi Beta Kappa Hall, the home of the campus theater, the ghost is of twentieth-century origin. Known as "Lucinda," the theater revenant is thought to be the spirit of a student who won the lead role in a production of Thornton Wilder's *Our Town*. In the stage drama, her character was to die and enter a netherworld from which she would watch the other characters play out their lives. Just two weeks before opening night, Lucinda was killed in an automobile accident. Since her death, her spirit, much like the character she was to play, has watched over activities in the theater building.

Late one night in the early 1970s, a music student prepared to gather up his music after practicing at a piano in Phi Beta Kappa Hall for an upcoming recital. Suddenly, he heard the voice of a young woman exclaim, "Oh, don't stop!" Cognizant that he was by himself in the auditorium, the young man turned on all of the lights and looked about to discover who had spoken the words.

Just about the time he made his way into the scene room under the stage, the entire building went dark and the door slammed behind him. Over the course of what seemed an interminable time, the terrified young man literally felt his way out of the spooky place into the welcome darkness of night.

Some theater students have heard the soft laugh of a woman echoing through the empty seats. On one occasion, an old, broken pipe organ that had not worked for years started playing by itself in a storage room under the stage.

Lucinda's ghost also manifests herself before the very eyes of the thespians. Following a rehearsal for a musical a few years ago, stagehands noticed that the lights in the lighting booth had mysteriously come on. From their vantage point, the two students clearly saw the spectral form of a young lady with black hair. She was wearing a white dress. In the flash of an eye, the booth went dark. Scampering from the stage, the young men separated and proceeded along the only two passages to the booth. En route, they passed no one, and they ultimately found the booth empty.

Three students anxious to encounter the theater wraith spent a dark, lonely night in the auditorium until they experienced a fright none of them would ever forget. From the orchestra pit, a sudden rush of cold wind engulfed the young men, who were positioned on the stage. It smelled musty, much like the air in a dark, dank crypt. As they fled the building, the breeze and its smell of death seemed to pursue them.

Perhaps the most frightening tale from the theater involves the white dress that Lucinda was to wear when the curtain opened. In the wake of the untimely death of the young actress, her understudy stepped forward to assume her role. At the final rehearsal on the eve of the opening, the replacement found it difficult to concentrate on her lines because she was overwhelmed by a sense that some invisible force was watching her. She looked out into the auditorium, which was empty save for a handful of theater students watching the rehearsal. But then the understudy saw something else. There on the third row, sitting upright in a seat, was the white dress she was to wear on the morrow.

Completed in 1733, the elegant, three-story, brick President's Home is the most famous haunted building on the campus. Like the Wren Building, this Queen Anne-style edifice was sequestered for use as a hospital to treat American and French casualties at the Battle of Yorktown. Not only has the majestic dwelling housed every president of William and Mary, it has also played host to some of the great luminaries of early American history, including George Washington, Benjamin Franklin, Thomas Jefferson, Patrick Henry, and James Madison. Nevertheless, the ghosts in residence here may be from a different era. When Union forces took control of Williamsburg during the Civil War, they promptly put the stately house to a rather mundane use. It served as a prison for captured Southern soldiers. Many tried to escape, and some are still trying.

For decades, strange, inexplicable sounds have been noted throughout the house by various college presidents and their families. Phantom footsteps are heard on the second and third floors. Doors and windows open and close at will. Long recognized by townspeople as a haunted house containing tortured souls, the dwelling is said to have a pervasive eerie feeling about it.

A visit to the campus of William and Mary will provide you with a wonderful opportunity to travel back into the distant past of America. Here, you will see college buildings that were standing on the very day that George Washington was born. And you might just encounter a ghost or two from various periods in the nation's haunted history.

For the Love of Daisy

Located just north of Lynchburg in Virginia's beautiful, historic Shenandoah Valley, Sweet Briar College celebrated its centennial anniversary in 2001. Female students attend classes on a 3,250-acre campus located on what were once the plantation sites of the Williams and Fletcher families.

Indiana Fletcher Williams donated the land for Sweet Briar to memorialize her daughter, Daisy, who died as a teenager in the late nineteenth century. On Monument Hill, a cemetery on a summit overlooking the Sweet Briar campus, the graves of Mrs. Williams—or "Indie," as she is affectionately referred to at the college—and Daisy can be found, along with those of other family members. But Indie and Daisy apparently are not at rest there. For as long as anyone can remember, the ghosts of mother and daughter have kept a vigil at "their" college.

Daisy Williams was only sixteen years old when she died in New York City in 1884. Her heartbroken parents decided that her body should be transported to Amherst County, Virginia, for burial on the family's ancestral grounds. Folks familiar with the marker surmounting Daisy's grave claim that it "screams" on occasion with a voice so loud that the sound carries down Monument Hill and spreads all over the campus.

One of Daisy's favorite haunts at the college is the Sweet Briar House, the former plantation mansion that now serves as the home of the school's president. When the first faculty members were hired at Sweet Briar, they were invited to live in the old plantation house because of a housing shortage in the area. No sooner did the professors move in than they experienced a supernatural presence in the place. One evening, an instructor was reading in the west parlor. A floor lamp adjacent to his large green velvet chair offered ample lighting. Suddenly, however, the exquisite crystal chandelier hanging overhead switched on by itself. Then it switched off. A half-dozen times, the light mysteriously went on and off.

Cognizant that there was no other human being in the room, the professor called out, "Daisy, stop playing with the lights!" The strange activity ceased immediately.

During Daisy's lifetime, one of her favorite pastimes was dancing and cavorting with her friends in front of the six pier mirrors that adorned the parlor of the Sweet Briar House. Elizabeth Robertson Lee, one of Daisy's chums, recalled their play in the house: "We would dance and pirouette in front of the tall mirrors in the parlor because we could see our reflections multiplied so many times. After we played, Mrs. Williams would give us cakes and sweets. It was like a fairy-tale castle, and Daisy was the princess. We did love to dance before the mirrors."

Many years after Daisy's death, another professor who lived in the house stopped at one of the parlor mirrors to adjust her hat. Upon looking into the mirror, she saw that it was cloudy. Perhaps the staff had not cleaned it, she thought. But upon closer inspection, the cloudiness disappeared. And then it returned, moving across the glass like a white mist.

Again it vanished, and then it came back. To the professor's eyes, the mysterious cloud seemed to be dancing!

Indie Williams died in 1900. Her ghost has long made appearances in the Sweet Briar House. Signora Hollins, who worked as a cook for the school in its early days, saw Indie's apparition on a number of occasions. On one particular autumn day in 1916, Indie's ghost informed Signora that the silver from the mansion was hidden in a bedroom wall near the landing of the front staircase. When the cook relayed the information to Emilie W. McVey, the president of Sweet Briar, carpenters were promptly summoned. When they opened the wall, they found three tightly wrapped bundles of silver.

In more recent times, a Sweet Briar alumna spent countless hours of research in an attempt to determine if a photographic likeness of Indie Williams existed. As she pored over her work at Sweet Briar House one day, she discovered that she had indeed located a photo of the college's founder. Excited by her find, the lady was anxious to share the good news with a friend she thought to be in the room with her. "Do you know who we have here?" she asked. "It is the founder, Miss Indie. We have found Miss Indie!"

When no one responded to her revelation, the woman looked around to find the room empty. But over her left shoulder, she heard a distinct laugh of satisfaction.

Sweet Briar House is not the only campus building haunted by Miss Indie, Daisy, or both. Three days before the school's gym was dedicated in 1931, college officials decided that it would be called the Daisy Williams Gymnasium. On the morning of the decision, the director of residence halls was working in a storage area at Gray Hall when she came upon a rather large bronze medallion that bore the bust of Daisy Williams. An employee of the college for some twenty-five years, the lady was familiar with every item in the storage room. But she had never seen this thing before. Sixteen inches in diameter, the framed medallion was mounted on a moth-damaged velvet background.

Cognizant of the hoopla surrounding the new gym, the lady promptly delivered the piece to Meta Glass, the president of Sweet Briar.

Subsequent inquiries about the medallion produced no answer to the mystery. At the dedication ceremony, President Glass noted, "I could think of no explanation of its appearance except that Miss Indie sent it in appreciation."

Daisy, it seems, enjoys working in the Mary Helen Cochran Library, particularly during the late evening. After the building is closed to the public, librarians often hear books mysteriously fall from shelves, phantom footsteps in the empty hallways, chairs being moved, and doors that open and close at will.

After turning the lights off and locking the library late one night, a student employee headed across campus toward her room. When she looked back toward the library, she could see that every light in the building was burning brightly.

On another night, a student studying in her dorm meticulously combed through her papers in a desperate search for a badly needed outline. She suddenly realized that she had left it at the library. But the hour was late—approximately two in the morning. A call to the campus police enabled the girl to gain after-hours access to the library. As the student, a library employee, and a campus security officer made their way down the steps toward the stacks, the officer used his flashlight to show the way. After a fruitless search for the outline, the trio decided to leave. Mysteriously, the lights came on.

Back at her dorm, the frustrated student found her outline on her desk, which she had thoroughly searched some twenty times prior to her late-night visit to the library.

Daisy's spirit is active in the Sweet Briar dorms as well. Residents in Meta Glass Hall and Reid Hall frequently report that items have vanished from their locked rooms. Lights go on and off as if they have a will of their own. The sound of human breathing, as if someone has just run up several flights of steps, has awakened more than one dorm resident.

The unexplained sounds emanating from the attic of Meta Glass Hall are attributed to Daisy's ghost. Several Sweet Briar students unwittingly took an eerie elevator ride to the attic on an evening in the mid-1990s. Nothing seemed out of the ordinary as the car made its way toward the third floor. Then the elevator stopped with a jolt. Try as they might, the girls could not make the door open. From the other side of it came a strange laugh. Acting on the belief that a fellow student was playing a prank on them, the trapped girls urged the trickster to let them out. No one responded.

After several nerve-racking minutes, the distressed young ladies used the elevator telephone to call the campus police. When assistance arrived, the officer informed the students that he would have to use a crowbar to free them because the door was stuck. At length, they were freed, only to be shocked at their location. The car had stopped at the attic. A special key was necessary to allow the elevator to travel to the attic. No one in the car had that key. And what about the laugh they had heard?

Neither of the ghosts at Sweet Briar has caused physical harm to anyone on the campus. But a bizarre incident experienced by two students and their male friends on Monument Hill in the mid-1990s should serve as a warning to those who would visit Daisy's grave late at night.

One evening about midnight, the foursome drove up to Monument Hill. There, one of the students stopped the automobile, put it in park, applied the emergency brake, and warned her riders that she was leaving with or without them in five minutes. After making their way through the creaky entrance gate, they were examining Daisy's grave when one of the young men asked if Sweet Briar students did anything special to honor Daisy. In jest, the driver said rather irreverently, "Yeah, we have to face the monument four times a day and bow."

No sooner had the words left her mouth than they all noticed that the car was moving down the hill. One of the males, fleet of foot, caught up with the vehicle, jumped in, and stopped it without damage or injury. To his amazement, the transmission was in drive and the emergency brake was off.

Indie Williams saw Sweet Briar College as a way to perpetuate the memory of her dear daughter, Daisy, who had died at such a tender age. At this picturesque campus in the mountains of Virginia, Daisy and her mom are far more than faded memories. Just ask anyone who has experienced their ghosts.

Jefferson's Haunted Academical Village

After establishing himself as one of the greatest statesmen that his nation would ever know, Thomas Jefferson came home to Charlottesville, where he set about creating a great university for his native state in 1819. In accordance with Jefferson's design, the University of Virginia was constructed to be an "academical village," a place where shared learning would infuse daily life.

Were Jefferson now able to walk the picturesque grounds of his university, which is consistently ranked among the best public schools of higher learning in the United States, he would no doubt be proud that his dream has been realized. And during his visit, the third American president would surely encounter the spectres that have called the university home for many years.

Central to Jefferson's university was its library. And so, at the head of the famed "Lawn" at the University of Virginia, he designed and erected the Rotunda. From its completion in 1826 until the Alderman Library was dedicated in 1938, the dome-shaped building served as the university library. During that 112-year span, a ghost took up residence in the Rotunda and remained there until the library collection was relocated to Alderman. When the books were moved, the ghost went with them.

Veteran library employees believe that the ghost is that of Bennett Wood Green, a former Confederate surgeon who bequeathed his extensive collection of books to the university. Despite the generosity of Green's bequest, it soon became all too apparent to university librarians that Green, or his ghost, did not want to part with his literary holdings, which were originally housed in the Dome Room of the Rotunda. Students and employees reported feeling that they were being watched when no one was about. It was as if someone or something were guarding the books.

The new library was named for Edwin Alderman, who in 1904 became the first person to hold the title of president of the university. When the Green Collection was carefully transported to its new location, Dr. Green's spirit attended the move. Once the books were carefully shelved, the ghost found a permanent home. Since that time, there have been numerous reports of a supernatural presence in the Alderman stacks.

Some staffers have become spooked while working in the stacks when the library was closed. When no other person was around, workers, much like those in the former library, sensed that someone was monitoring their activities. Most of the experiences took place just after midnight.

During late-night study sessions in the vicinity of the Green Collection, more than one student has seen out of the corner of his eye a spectral figure moving about. Upon closer examination, there was nothing or no one to be found. Other students have heard the echoes of footsteps behind them as they wandered the stacks in search of particular volumes. Their quick glances behind have never revealed a human presence.

When such paranormal encounters are reported to library personnel, they are usually attributed to Dr. Green. That is, unless the spooky experiences take place in the Garnett Room. There, the spectre is that of another admirer and protector of fine books.

Among the outstanding acquisitions for the Alderman Library when it opened was the Garnett Collection. In addition to the impressive collection of some twelve hundred antiquarian volumes and various furnishings from the antebellum period, the acquisition included the ghost of a nineteenth-century physician who had once spent countless hours perusing the Garnett books when they were housed at Elmwood, a spectacular mansion on the bank of the Rappahannock River near Fredericksburg.

Elmwood, constructed just before the Revolutionary War, was the home of Muscoe Russell Hunter Garnett—a distinguished alumnus of the University of Virginia—from 1821 until his death in 1864. Among the many guests entertained by the Garnett family was a physician who quickly developed a great fondness for the Elmwood library. On the last of his many visits over a forty-year period, the doctor died of natural causes and was interred on the plantation grounds.

Following Muscoe Garnett's death from typhoid near the end of the Civil War, the grand estate was abandoned. But no harm came to the library over the next three-quarters of a century while the place was devoid of human occupation. And for good reason!

Throughout the surrounding countryside, folks reported that the doctor emerged from his grave every night and laid claim to his favorite chamber and the library in the mansion. The physician's ghost was said to have even dusted the much-cherished books.

When the Garnett heirs donated the priceless assemblage of books and antiques to the University of Virginia, the spectral caretaker made himself at home in the room at Alderman designed to house the collection. He remains there to this day, lending supernatural assistance to the security and custodial employees at the library.

Thomas Jefferson saw his university as a place built upon honor and integrity. One of the most famous ghosts on the Charlottesville campus was instrumental in establishing the school's tradition of honor, the very framework upon which life at the University of Virginia rests.

When John Anthony Gardner Davis accepted an appointment as law professor, the university was less than twenty years old. Married to the niece of Thomas Jefferson, Davis quickly won respect on the campus and became chairman of the faculty. But this was at a time when students were openly attacking and assaulting their professors.

On the night of November 13, 1840, the distinct sound of gunshots emanating from the Lawn drew Davis from his quarters at nearby Pavilion X, a residential apartment in Jefferson's original campus design. On the campus green, two masked students—later revealed to be Joseph G. Semmes and Willaim A. Kincaid—were firing pistols.

Anxious to quell the disturbance, the professor approached Semmes. According to Peter Carr, Davis's nephew, "Davis stepped up to him & caught hold of his disguise in order to detect him, as he was committing a high infringement of the laws of good order of the Institution. The person however jerked away from him, ran three or four yards, wheeled around, and fired his pistol at Mr. Davis." Severely wounded in the abdomen, Davis died two days later.

In the aftermath of the murder, Semmes returned to his native Georgia and committed suicide.

Henry St. George Tucker, who succeeded Davis as professor of law, was anxious for the university community to atone for the tragic and unnecessary death of the esteemed faculty member. He promptly went to work to eradicate the widespread misbehavior on campus, earlier described by Jefferson as "vicious irregularities." His efforts culminated in the adoption of the university's famed honor system in 1842.

As for George Davis, his ghost is said to linger in the vicinity of Jefferson and Seventh Streets in Charlottesville. Eugene Davis, the professor's oldest son, once lived in a house near the intersection of the two streets. Occupants of the dwelling have never seen Davis's ghost, but they have heard disembodied footsteps and the phantom opening of the gate latch late at night.

Although the ghost of the father of the University of Virginia has never been witnessed on the Charlottesville campus, the "spirit" of Thomas Jefferson is very much in evidence at this historic seat of learning. Perhaps his ghost is not needed here, for there are spectral guardians of the two things that were of tantamount importance to Jefferson at his university—its library and its honor.

VIRGINIA MILITARY INSTITUTE
LEXINGTON, VIRGINIA

Ghosts of a Military Kind

The history of Lexington, Virginia, is inexorably linked to matters military. Buried here are Robert E. Lee and Thomas Jonathan "Stonewall" Jackson, two of the most respected generals that America has produced. And long prominent in Lexington is Virginia Military Institute, the oldest state-supported military college in the United States. Since 1839, cadets have received academic and military training in the hallowed halls and on the historic grounds of this renowned school. And over its many years of operation, V.M.I. has acquired a most haunted heritage.

Cadet life has long been centered around the famous V.M.I. Barracks. Designed by noted nineteenth-century American architect Alexander

Jackson Davis (1803-92), the Barracks are part of the first American college campus planned entirely in the Gothic Revival style. Their turrets and towers are reminiscent of Europe's medieval castles and cathedrals. They look as if they are haunted—and indeed they are.

Some thirteen hundred cadets attend V.M.I. today. All cadets, male and female (women were first admitted in 1997), are required to live in the Barracks. Running under these castlelike structures is an underground netherworld known as "the Catacombs." The strange, mysterious noises coming from the dark, dank cellars have never been satisfactorily explained. Neither has the frightening presence that has terrified many courageous cadets living in the Barracks. Known as "the Yellow Peril," the otherworldly thing is said to have a hideous yellow face with a scar that bleeds.

Cadets first encountered the haunting years ago when a freshman—commonly called a "Rat" on campus—was directed to occupy the room of a junior until the upperclassman returned. However, the Rat was not in the assigned room when the junior opened the door. Upon being dressed down and called on to provide an explanation for his insubordination, the first-year student was in such a frightened state that he could hardly speak. In his almost incoherent ramblings, the highly agitated fellow tried to describe the terrifying thing he had heard crawling under the floorboards. Although they were highly skeptical of the story, his fellow cadets searched the crawlspace under the floor. They found nothing.

Three days later, however, a group of cadets observed the now-infamous Yellow Peril as it peered through a window. They described it as a nonhuman entity that seemed to be in search of something or someone.

No one knows what the Yellow Peril is or from whence it came. But one thing is for sure: the awful spectre has terrified every student who has witnessed it. After encountering the mysterious haunt, some cadets from China left the Lexington campus, never to return.

Cadets who fail to meet the academic standards and code of discipline at V.M.I. are "drummed out" of the college prior to graduation. When a student is forced to leave the corps under such circumstances, the flags on the Barracks are said to suddenly and mysteriously stand out straight, as if blown by a strong wind.

On the historic parade grounds, cadets spend innumerable hours standing watch. Throughout the school's long history, countless student sentries have encountered unidentified ghosts roaming about. A spectral figure hanging from a tree has frequently been witnessed.

Jackson Memorial Hall, dedicated to the memory of Stonewall Jackson, was completed in 1915 with funds appropriated by the federal government to compensate V.M.I. for the damage it suffered during the Civil War. Upon entering the magnificent three-story Gothic Revival building, which now serves as a campus museum, visitors are immediately awed by a spectacular oil painting by Benjamin West Clinedinst (class of 1880) that depicts the famous charge of the corps of cadets in the Battle of New Market.

On May 15, 1864, Confederate major general John Breckinridge had no alternative but to send into battle some 250 teenage cadets from V.M.I., who had marched eighty miles north from Lexington to thwart the Union incursion into "the Breadbasket of the Confederacy." At the height of the battle, the student soldiers joined the Sixty-second Virginia in a fearless charge across a rain-soaked field that literally sucked off their shoes. When the Battle of New Market was over, the cadets proudly marched back to V.M.I. as the heroes of the dramatic victory. Ten of their comrades had paid the ultimate price. A half-dozen of the bodies were buried on the V.M.I. campus.

Clinedinst's moving artwork captures the spirit and drama of the legendary charge at New Market. It's almost as if the battle comes to life. Sometimes, it actually does. Cadets who have been alone in Jackson Memorial Hall have experienced the strange things that go on in the painting after the building is closed. Mysteriously, the fighting cadets begin to move across the landscape of Bushong's farm, and the guns thunder and flash fire.

One of the young cadets who took part in and survived the Battle of New Market was Moses Jacob Ezekial (1844-1917). The first Jew to attend and graduate from V.M.I., Ezekial subsequently became the most respected American-born sculptor of his time. So impressed was Robert E. Lee with the multitalented Jewish cadet that he counseled him, "I hope you will be an artist, as it seems to me you are cut out for one. But whatever you do, try to prove to the world that if we did not succeed in our struggle, we are worthy of success, and do earn a reputation in whatever profession you undertake."

Two of Ezekial's masterpieces are tangible evidence that the cadet followed the advice of the great general. Both stand near Jackson Memorial Hall, and both are haunted.

All who behold *Virginia Mourning Her Dead* are moved by the grandeur of the bronze statue of a weeping woman that surmounts the graves of the six cadets interred here after they gave their lives at New Market. Some people have reported that the monument is more than symbolic. Actual tears have been observed flowing from the metal eyes, and moans have been heard from the mouth of the statue.

Not very far from the graves stands the other Ezekial piece. It is an unusual likeness of Stonewall Jackson wearing a slouch hat.

No name in the history of V.M.I. is more beloved and revered than that of Jackson. From the time he was hired as a professor of natural philosophy, optics, and artillery tactics in 1851 until his death a dozen years later, the West Point-educated Jackson was dedicated to the cadets at the Lexington school. Long before they did battle at New Market, the student soldiers had twice marched into action behind their highly eccentric but much-admired professor. Jackson led them first at Harpers Ferry in 1859 during the apprehension of John Brown. Then he marched with them as their commander to Richmond when Virginia joined the Confederacy. In 1863, at the onset of the Battle of Chancellorsville, which would prove to be Jackson's greatest and last field victory, the general proudly exclaimed, "The Institute will be heard from today!"

When a cadet is drummed out of V.M.I., the tradition is that fellow cadets turn their backs on the student who has dishonored the school. Those familiar with the statue of Jackson say that another stretch mark appears on its bronze neck every time a cadet leaves V.M.I. in disgrace. Jackson's likeness is said to turn its head in disgust.

After Jackson died on May 10, 1863, his body was transported to Lexington for burial. Prior to interment, it was placed in state in Jackson's old classroom under dignified cadet guard. Outside, the general's well-trained artillery students offered cannon salutes from sunrise to sunset. Then he was buried in the Lexington cemetery that today bears his name. But Stonewall's spirit is very much alive at the school he loved. When an ill word is spoken about V.M.I., the air suddenly rushes out of the building where Jackson lectured his young protégés.

Few college campuses can boast a military history and tradition comparable to that of Virginia Military Institute. And what school has more ghosts related to the art of war than does V.M.I.?

Senators, Sisters, and Spectres

Tucked away on a picturesque 170-acre campus overlooking the city of Elkins, West Virginia, Davis and Elkins College bears the names of the two men who founded the liberal-arts school at the dawn of the twentieth century. Henry Gassaway Davis and Stephen Benton Elkins not only gave their names to the institution but also left behind their fabulous mansions, now the most historic buildings at the college. Ghosts, some of which are thought to represent ladies very closely related to Davis and Elkins, inhabit the spectacular former summer homes that stand within sight of each other.

Though they pledged their political allegiance to different parties,

Henry Davis and Stephen Elkins had much in common. During Reconstruction, they became business partners and developed the first railroad to the wild and rugged mountains of eastern West Virginia. This enterprise enabled them to successfully market the vast coal and timber reserves of the Alleghenies. Their personal relationship was cemented in 1877, when Elkins married one of Davis's daughters.

In the heart of their business empire, the two entrepreneurs founded the town of Elkins. There, in 1890, Stephen Elkins began the construction of a magnificent summer home patterned after a Rhineland castle admired by his wife, Hallie Davis Elkins. In her honor, Elkins named the mansion Halliehurst. A year later, Henry Davis commenced building his grand summer estate on a 360-acre tract just west of Halliehurst. Initially, he called the place Mingo Moor, but the name was soon changed to Graceland to honor his youngest daughter, Grace.

Meanwhile, the two business tycoons broadened their sphere of influence.

After serving in the West Virginia legislature in the years immediately following the Civil War, Henry Davis was elected to two terms in the United States Senate. A powerful Democrat, he chaired the Appropriations Committee in the Forty-sixth Congress. In 1904, Davis was the Democratic nominee for vice president of the United States.

Like his father-in-law, Stephen Elkins served in the United States Senate. After his tenure as secretary of war in the Benjamin Harrison administration, Elkins was elected in 1895 to the first of his three terms in the Senate. When he died in office in 1911, his son, Davis Elkins—the grandson of Henry Davis—was appointed to the seat.

In 1904, Henry Davis and his son-in-law joined forces to establish a Presbyterian-affiliated college on the south side of Elkins. Fire destroyed the original campus less than twenty years later. But thanks to the generosity of the families of Henry Davis and Stephen Elkins, their two sprawling summer estates formed the nucleus of a new campus.

Today, the two expansive mansions are said to be haunted by the women for whom they were named.

Graceland, noted for its refined elegance, is currently used by the college as an inn and conference center. The tall, imposing edifice was constructed of native timber and stone. Among the most striking features of the thirty-five-room mansion are its Tiffany windows and two-story great hall, which measures sixty feet by twenty-eight feet.

Following the death of her mother in 1902, Grace Davis—said to be Senator Davis's favorite daughter—assumed the role of hostess of the house. When Senator Davis died in 1916, she and her husband continued to summer at the estate. Grace was killed in an automobile accident in 1931. Some ten years later, the stately house was presented to Davis and Elkins College, which used it for student housing until 1970.

Over the years, numerous supernatural occurrences in the building have been reported. Students, employees, and visitors have heard a variety of eerie, unexplained noises throughout the rambling structure. From Grace's third-floor bedroom—which featured a porch where she could dry her hair in the sun after washing it—to the great hall, occupants of Graceland have been overwhelmed by the odd feeling that they were being watched or followed by an unseen force. On one occasion, a prom held in the great hall was ended abruptly after many of the attendees were spooked. Speculation is that Grace remains in residence here in spirit form. Many of the bizarre sounds are attributed to her.

But local legend has it that another supernatural presence is the source of some of the creepy goings-on at Graceland. A former servant was reportedly buried under the earthen floor of the basement. His ghost is said to roam the place where he once worked.

Just up the hill from Graceland stands Halliehurst. From outward appearances, Graceland looks to be a mysterious, sturdy stone mansion, while Halliehurst has all the trappings of a haunted house, thanks to its towers, tall chimneys, and sweeping porches. Wood siding and shakes cover the exterior of the enormous three-story building, which is surmounted by the largest shingled roof in the state.

From the day it was completed in 1890 until it was conveyed to the college in 1923, Halliehurst was the domain of Hallie Davis Elkins, the only woman in American history to have been a daughter, wife, and mother of United States senators. Based upon some of the scary things that have gone on in the mansion since Hallie gave it to the college, some people are convinced that Halliehurst remains the domain of her ghost.

Once the rambling estate and the surrounding sixty acres were donated to the college and the campus was relocated to the site, Halliehurst was used alternately for women's housing and administrative offices until World War II, when it and other campus buildings were sequestered for military training purposes. Once peace was restored, the mansion served as a dormitory, the president's office, and a fallout shelter until the 1960s.

Throughout this initial forty-year period of college ownership, Halliehurst acquired its haunted reputation. Students residing in the house were terrified by the sights and sounds they experienced. Frequently, a spectral entity snuck up on unwitting students. At other times, something could be heard running up and down an empty staircase. No rational explanation being available to account for the eerie presence, the haunt was attributed to Hallie.

Some student residents of the mansion had very personal encounters with Hallie's ghost.

Two sorority sisters who shared a suite in Halliehurst either disbelieved or had no respect for the abiding spirit. One day, the young women taunted the ghost when they opened the door to the chamber that once belonged to Hallie, yelling, "We hope we didn't disturb you, Hallie!" There was no time to enjoy their mirth, for as soon as they closed the door, it opened on its own. Concern erasing their smiles, they cautiously peered into the room, which was devoid of human occupants. Before they could flee, the door abruptly slammed shut.

One coed considered by her peers to be somewhat self-centered and eccentric beat a hasty retreat from the parlor on an otherwise splendid afternoon. The screaming girl told her fellow students that the spectral form of Hallie had ordered her to leave Halliehurst.

In the late 1960s, the massive structure was deemed to be a safety hazard. For a time, it was abandoned to the elements—and to the spirits in residence. Weeds, shadows, and cobwebs soon added to the haunted aura of Halliehurst.

During this period of vacancy, college security regularly monitored the place, particularly at night, to ensure that students and other curiosity seekers did not make their way into the structure. In the mid-1970s, a watchman and his son were taking a break in a first-floor room after thoroughly checking every portion of the house in the wee morning hours. Suddenly, they heard distinct female voices, as if some women were walking up from the basement. Perplexed by the sounds, the men scrambled toward the steps, where they fully expected to surprise the intruders. No humans were found, nor was there any sign of forced entry into Halliehurst.

A subsequent fund-raising campaign enabled the college to return the spectacular Victorian edifice to much of its original grandeur. Now, it houses offices for the president and the admissions staff. Meetings and receptions are frequently held in Hallie's grand house. While her ghost has not often been seen in recent times, her presence is apparent. On more than one occasion, people in the house have been restrained from falling down steps or over a balcony by an unseen force. Several persons, on the other hand, have experienced an invisible push, though no one has fallen. On some occasions, various objects in the house have mysteriously disappeared and remained "lost" for days, only to reappear in their original places.

Both Halliehurst and Graceland are open to the public. You are welcome to marvel at the magnificent architecture and workmanship in these two campus gems, both National Historic Landmarks. You can also make reservations to sleep and eat at Graceland. But whether you choose to see these castles in the dark of night or the light of day, you'll probably feel that you are being watched by the spirits of Davis and Elkins. After all, they are the ladies—or the ghosts—of the houses.

Spooky Mountaineers

Located at Morgantown in northern West Virginia, some seventy miles south of Pittsburgh, West Virginia University boasts a student body of more than twenty-one thousand, making it the largest university in the state. And by all accounts, the school also has the largest population of ghosts of any college in the Mountaineer State.

Elizabeth Moore Hall, situated in the heart of the main campus, is home to the most well-documented spook. Constructed in 1928 and listed on the National Register of Historic Places, the tall, majestic brick edifice is said to be haunted by the woman for whom it was named. Elizabeth Moore (1830-1930), the dean of female education in West Virginia, was a stalwart supporter of women students on the Morgantown campus after West Virginia University became coeducational in 1889. Recent reports of supernatural activities in the Colonial-style building indicate that she is still at work in "spirit."

Brenda Eli, who worked as a receptionist and secretary in Elizabeth Moore Hall from 1980 until 1992, first experienced the ghost on a cold evening in the early 1980s. At the end of one particular workday, Mrs. Eli was making ready to leave for home. She had turned out all of the lights, save one in the foyer. With her back to that light, Mrs. Eli began putting on her coat and gloves in the otherwise dark room. Suddenly, she felt a gentle breeze that caused her to turn around. There, she saw the spectre of a lady attired in a long black dress and black boots of the style worn in the early twentieth century. In a flash, the apparition faded away at the very wall where Elizabeth Moore's portrait was hanging. Certain that she had just witnessed the wraith of the noted educator, the spooked secretary hastily exited the building into the chilly night.

Over time, Mrs. Eli came to appreciate the presence of Mrs. Moore's abiding spirit. While working late at night in the building, she never felt threatened. On the contrary, she believed that the ghost was there to protect her.

Mrs. Eli was not the only person to encounter the revenant in Elizabeth Moore Hall. Custodial staff members have noted that the portrait of Mrs. Moore has been mysteriously rearranged during the early-morning hours on a number of occasions. From the time the after-hours custodian leaves the building at two in the morning until the next custodian reports for duty three hours later, the position of the portrait of Elizabeth Moore has changed. No one has been in the building to make the switch. Apparently, the ghost is insistent that the portrait of Mrs. Moore hang in one particular spot.

Sue Rubinstein, the former director of orientation, has also encountered the supernatural presence of Mrs. Moore in the building. As she worked late one night, Rubinstein heard what turned out to be a phantom knock at a closed door and observed curtains blowing at a closed window when there was no breeze in the room. Then every button on her telephone suddenly lit up, even though there were no incoming calls.

Other employees have reported seeing the ghost of Mrs. Moore floating over the building's swimming pool.

Across the main campus at Boreman Hall are several spooks of unknown origin. Boreman North, the newer of the two sections of the residence hall, is home to 230 female students. Numerous residents of the fourth floor have heard eerie, frightening noises above their rooms, though there are only four floors in the building.

In one Boreman North room, two coeds were startled from their sleep when a well-secured door mirror suddenly fell and shattered without any apparent cause. Thereafter, the girls witnessed the shadow of what appeared to be a small head on the wall of their room.

In another room at Boreman North, a young lady was applying her makeup one morning when the spectral form of an old woman walked through the closed door and into her room, only to disappear in an instant.

A member of the dorm's cleaning staff woke every sleeping student on one floor with a shriek of terror early one morning when she heard unearthly sounds and saw eerie shadows in an otherwise vacant corridor.

Over at the Beta Psi chapter house of the Beta Theta Pi fraternity, the brothers share their quarters with a ghost that often clangs chains in the lower portion of the structure. Some claim that the ghost is that of the butler who served the fraternity members in the 1940s. Others believe the revenant is of more sinister origin. A homeless person said to have been permitted to live in the basement of the house in the 1980s committed suicide by hanging himself in a hallway. Now, phantom sounds emanate from that very spot.

Beyond a doubt, the most grisly ghost tale from West Virginia University began on January 28, 1970, when two coeds were picked up by an unknown motorist outside of the Mining Engineering Building. Their decapitated bodies were discovered three months later near Cheat Lake, then a popular student hangout located northeast of the campus. Their heads were never found, nor was the perpetrator of the ghastly crime ever brought to justice.

Since the murders, motorists driving late at night along the highway near the site where the corpses were discovered have been distracted by the blurry apparitions of two girls coming forth from the woods.

If on a foggy night you happen to be hopelessly lost en route to Morgantown, keep a close lookout for these two headless ghosts. They are either looking for their missing heads or trying to get back to school. At any rate, the sight of them will assure you that you are on Route 857, a road that leads to the other spooks of West Virginia University.